HYDROSPHERE

Freshwater Systems and Pollution

OUR FRAGILE PLANET

Atmosphere

Biosphere

Climate

Geosphere

Humans and the Natural Environment

Hydrosphere

Oceans

Polar Regions

HYDROSPHERE

Freshwater Systems and Pollution

DANA DESONIE, PH.D.

CHELSEA HOUSE
PUBLISHERS
An imprint of Infobase Publishing

Hydrosphere

Copyright © 2008 by Dana Desonie, Ph.D.

Chelsea House
An imprint of Infobase Publishing
132 West 31st Street
New York NY 10001

Library of Congress Cataloging-in-Publication Data
Desonie, Dana.
    Hydrosphere : freshwater systems and pollution / Dana Desonie.
        p. cm. — (Our fragile planet)
    Includes bibliographical references and index.
    ISBN-13: 978-0-8160-6215-7 (hardcover)
    ISBN-10: 0-8160-6215-3 (hardcover)
    1. Water—Pollution—Environmental aspects—Juvenile literature. 2. Water—Pollution—Health aspects—Juvenile literature. 3. Fresh water—Juvenile literature. 4. Water—Purification—Juvenile literature. I. Title. II. Series.
    QH545.W3D47 2007
    551.48--dc22   2007022398

Text design by Annie O'Donnell
Cover design by Ben Peterson

Printed in the United States of America

Bang NMSG 10 9 8 7 6 5 4 3 2 1

This book is printed on acid-free paper.

Cover photograph: Corbis Royalty Free/age fotostock

Contents

Preface

The planet is a marvelous place: a place with blue skies, wild storms, deep lakes, and rich and diverse ecosystems. The tides ebb and flow, baby animals are born in the spring, and tropical rain forests harbor an astonishing array of life. The Earth sustains living things and provides humans with the resources to maintain a bountiful way of life: water, soil, and nutrients to grow food, and the mineral and energy resources to build and fuel modern society, among many other things.

The physical and biological sciences provide an understanding of the whys and hows of natural phenomena and processes—why the sky is blue and how metals form, for example—and insights into how the many parts are interrelated. Climate is a good example. Among the many influences on the Earth's climate are the circulation patterns of the atmosphere and the oceans, the abundance of plant life, the quantity of various gases in the atmosphere, and even the sizes and shapes of the continents. Clearly, to understand climate it is necessary to have a basic understanding of several scientific fields and to be aware of how these fields are interconnected.

As Earth scientists like to say, the only thing constant about our planet is change. From the ball of dust, gas, and rocks that came together 4.6 billion years ago to the lively and diverse globe that orbits the Sun today, very little about the Earth has remained the same for long. Yet, while change is fundamental, people have altered the environment unlike any other species in Earth's history. Everywhere there are reminders of our presence. A look at the sky might show a sooty cloud or a jet contrail. A look at the sea might reveal plastic refuse, oil, or only a few fish swimming where once they had been countless. The land has been deforested and strip-mined. Rivers and lakes have been polluted. Changing conditions and habitats have caused some plants and animals to expand their populations, while others have become extinct. Even the climate—which for millennia was thought to be beyond human influence—has been shifting due to alterations in the makeup of atmospheric gases brought about by human activities. The planet is changing fast and people are the primary cause.

OUR FRAGILE PLANET is a set of eight books that celebrate the wonders of the world by highlighting the scientific processes behind them. The books also look at the science underlying the tremendous influence humans are having on the environment. The set is divided into volumes based on the large domains on which humans have had an impact: *Atmosphere, Climate, Hydrosphere, Oceans, Geosphere, Biosphere,* and *Polar Regions.* The volume *Humans and the Natural Environment* describes the impact of human activity on the planet and explores ways in which we can live more sustainably.

A core belief expressed in each volume is that to mitigate the impacts humans are having on the Earth, each of us must understand the scientific processes that operate in the natural world. We must understand how human activities disrupt those processes and use that knowledge to predict ways that changes in one system will affect seemingly unrelated systems. These books express the belief that science is the solid ground from which we can reach an agreement on the behavioral changes that we must adopt—both as individuals and as a society—to solve the problems caused by the impact of humans on our fragile planet.

Acknowledgments

I would like to thank, above all, the scientists who have dedicated their lives to the study of the Earth, especially those engaged in the important work of understanding how human activities are impacting the planet. Many thanks to the staff of Facts On File and Chelsea House for their guidance and editing expertise: Frank Darmstadt, Executive Editor; Brian Belval, Senior Editor; and Leigh Ann Cobb, independent developmental editor. Dr. Tobi Zausner located the color images that illustrate our planet's incredible beauty and the harsh reality of the effects human activities are having on it. Thanks also to my agent, Jodie Rhodes, who got me involved in this project.

Family and friends were a great source of support and encouragement as I wrote these books. Special thanks to the May '97 Moms, who provided the virtual water cooler that kept me sane during long days of writing. Cathy Propper was always enthusiastic as I was writing the books, and even more so when they were completed. My mother, Irene Desonie, took great care of me as I wrote for much of June 2006. Mostly importantly, my husband, Miles Orchinik, kept things moving at home when I needed extra writing time and provided love, support, and encouragement when I needed that, too. This book is dedicated to our children, Reed and Maya, who were always loving, and usually patient. I hope these books do a small bit to help people understand how their actions impact the future for all children.

Introduction

Planet Earth is unique in the solar system. No other planet has suitable conditions for the existence of abundant water. This irreplaceable substance can take the form of a liquid, solid, or vapor. Because water is present in each of these three states, it cycles through the Earth's atmosphere, glaciers and ice caps, streams and lakes, and even through living creatures. It is safe to say that without water, our planet would be lifeless.

When viewed from far out in the solar system, Earth appears as a blue dot. The blue is water, nearly all of which is seawater. Freshwater makes up only 3% of the water on the planet, and two thirds of that is trapped in glaciers and ice caps. This means that only 1% of the Earth's water is available—in sources such as lakes, rivers, and groundwater—to support rich ecosystems of plants and animals.

The small amount of freshwater that is found on Earth is invaluable to people. Water from inland waterways is used for drinking, bathing, and other domestic purposes. For millennia, people have depended on streams, ponds, and lakes for acquiring food; for raising plants and land animals; and for harvesting fish and other aquatic creatures. These days, aquaculture, also called fish farming, augments the amount of food that freshwater sources provide. Over time, inland waters have become important for industrial processes and power generation.

Freshwater has long been a valuable resource for commerce and industry. Before extensive roadways were built, and when air travel was just a fantasy, streams and lakes provided the easiest means of traveling into continental interiors. Settlements grew at the confluence of two streams or at a point where a river could be easily crossed, becoming the crossroads for people moving through the area. Materials could be shipped along the waterways as well; industries grew along rivers and lakes where water was used for transporting goods, powering factories, and disposing of industrial waste.

The waterways are useful to people for other reasons. Streams and lakes can be engineered to provide a year-round water source, to prevent flooding, and to supply electric power. While dams and levees provide useful services, their impact is not uniformly favorable. For instance, flood control decreases the nutrients that reach a stream's floodplain and the sediment that is needed to replenish wetlands. As water backs up behind a dam, it drowns a valley, perhaps displacing populations from their homes and livelihoods and often bringing about the loss of a beautiful natural or cultural resource.

People exploit the waterways by using them as a sink for their wastes. Waste can be emptied directly into streams and lakes, where it is assumed it will be diluted and dispersed, or it can enter by accident. Sewage, industrial waste, runoff from parking lots and roads, even waste heat from power plants and industrial plants, continue to pollute waters today. Air pollutants from oil, gasoline, and coal burning combine with water in the atmosphere to create acid rain, which changes the acidity of lakes, streams, and soils and causes ecosystem damage. Even living creatures can be pollutants if they are introduced to a new area. In some cases, these introduced species can take over a habitat and drive out the native species.

Some types of water pollution have decreased tremendously in the past few decades so that many waterways that were once toxic waste dumps are now much cleaner. Wastewater treatment plants have been very successful at treating sewage, although some plants are old or do not have the capacity to handle overflow from storms. Some pollutant sources, such as some industrial waste sites, have been or are being cleaned up so that their pollutants no longer reach the water. But chemicals with unknown effects on humans or wildlife are being added to water all the time on the assumption that small quantities are not harmful. This assumption has turned out not to be true with DDT and several other compounds. Once these toxins enter the environment, they are very difficult to remove. The result is that the waterways resemble a toxic soup that may be the cause of cancers and other illnesses in people and wildlife.

This book, *Hydrosphere*, describes human uses and abuses of inland waterways. Part One discusses the planet's fresh water and how people use it. Part Two looks at the myriad pollutants that are released into the environment and their effects on human health and ecosystems. Current methods that are used for cleaning up pollution and ideas for future cleanups are described in Part Three. The last chapter of Part Three traces the history of pollution in the Great Lakes as it represents the history of water pollution in the United States.

PART ONE

THE WATER PLANET

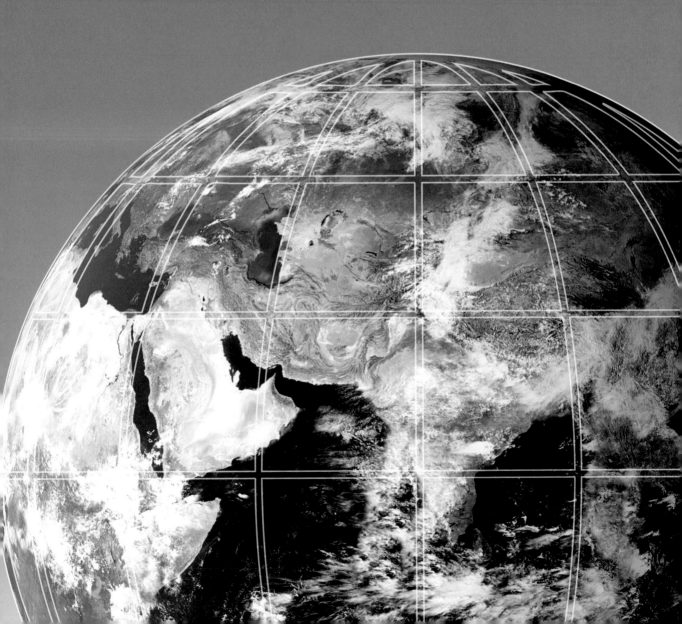

The Water Cycle

This chapter discusses water—the Earth's most distinctive nonliving feature. The pressure and temperature conditions on Earth allow liquid water to be stable; it is also abundant, a situation that is unique in the solar system. Water is also present as a gas, which is known as **water vapor**, and as solid ice. The Earth became cool enough for liquid water to form early in the planet's history. Under present conditions, the substance cycles between the atmosphere, oceans, and surface sources such as lakes, **streams**, and **groundwater**. Any water moving on the ground surface, from a rivulet to the world's largest river, is a stream. Groundwater is water that is found in rock or soil beneath the land surface. Most of these water **reservoirs** contain liquid water, although the atmosphere holds water vapor, and **glaciers** and **ice caps** hold water in the form of ice. A glacier is a moving mass of ice and snow that forms on land.

WHERE THE WATER IS

The Earth's **hydrosphere** contains all of the water found in its atmosphere, oceans, lakes, streams, and groundwater. Water is also found in animals and plants. A look at Earth from space shows that 97.5% of the Earth's water is in the oceans. This water is **saline** (salty), containing about 3.5% salt on average. **Brackish** water has salinity levels between freshwater and seawater and is found in saline lakes and estuaries. Only a tiny amount of the planet's water—the remaining 2.5%—is fresh. The table on page 5 shows the percentages of Earth's freshwater held in the planet's reservoirs. Most of this water is held in ice, permanent snow, and the permanently frozen soil known as **permafrost**.

THE WATER MOLECULE

Water has many unique properties stemming from the structure of the water molecule. The molecule's chemical formula is H_2O: two hydrogen atoms and one oxygen atom. To fully appreciate water's special properties, it is necessary to understand the basic chemistry of **atoms**, **molecules**, and **chemical bonding**.

Atoms, Molecules, and Chemical Bonding

An **atom** is the smallest unit of a chemical **element**—a substance that cannot be chemically reduced to simpler substances—that has the properties of that element. At an atom's center is a **nucleus**, containing **protons**, which have a small positive electrical charge, and **neutrons**, which have no charge. An atom's **atomic mass** is the sum of its protons and neutrons. A particular element, say potassium, will always have the same number of protons in its nucleus but may contain a different number of neutrons. For example, potassium always has 19 protons, but it can have an additional 20, 21, or 22 neutrons. Therefore, the atomic weight of a potassium nucleus can be 39, 40, or 41. Each different atomic weight creates a different **isotope** of potassium: potassium-39, potassium-40, or potassium-41.

The Percentage of Earth's Freshwater in Each of Its Reservoirs

WATER SOURCE	PERCENTAGE OF FRESHWATER*
Ice caps, glaciers, and permanent snow	68.7
Groundwater	30.1
Ground ice and permafrost	0.86
Lakes	0.26
Atmosphere	0.04
Freshwater wetlands (swamps)	0.03
Rivers	0.006
Biological water	0.003

*Due to rounding, the sum of these percentages is slightly less than 100%.

Source: Gleick, P. H. "Water Resources." In *Encyclopedia of Climate and Weather*, Vol. 2: 817–823. New York: Oxford University Press, 1996.

Electrons orbit the nucleus in shells; each electron has a small negative electrical charge. If the number of protons and electrons in an atom is equal, the atom has no charge. Atoms are most stable when their outer electron shells are full; and an atom will give, take, or share one or more electrons to achieve stability. An **ion** is an atom that has gained or lost an electron. If an atom loses an electron, it loses a negative charge, so it becomes a positive ion. If it gains an electron, it gains a negative charge and becomes a negative ion.

A molecule is the smallest unit of a compound that has all the properties of that compound. A molecule is made of more than one atom or ion and has no electrical charge. Chemical bonds allow ions to come together to form molecules. Bonds arise because unlike charges attract. In **covalent bonds**, an atom retains its own electrons but shares one or more of them with another atom so that each has a full outer electron shell. Covalent bonds are very strong bonds. In **ionic bonds**, one atom gives one or more electrons to another atom. **Molecular weight** is the sum of the weights of all of a molecule's atoms.

If the positive and negative charges in a molecule are not evenly distributed, and one side is positive and the other side is negative, the molecule is a **polar molecule**. The positive side of one polar molecule will be attracted to the negative side of another polar molecule, forming a **hydrogen bond**. These bonds are weak, only 4% as strong as covalent bonds.

The Water Molecule's Structure

Water is made of hydrogen and oxygen atoms that form a unique structure. Hydrogen is the smallest and simplest atom: one proton orbited by one electron. Oxygen has eight protons and eight orbiting electrons: two in its inner electron shell and six in its outer electron shell. Because oxygen's outer electron shell needs eight electrons to be full, the atom must acquire two more electrons. Hydrogen has one electron and needs either two or zero electrons to have either a full or empty outer shell. Two hydrogen atoms sharing their single electron with one oxygen atom create water (H_2O), and these covalent bonds make H_2O a very strong molecule. Water can break up into one hydrogen ion (H^+) and one hydroxyl ion (OH^-).

Water is a polar molecule, so water molecules are held together loosely by hydrogen bonds. These bonds greatly influence the structure of liquid and solid water. As water freezes into ice, the molecules form an open framework of 6-sided rings. The open air in the ring

(A) A water molecule consists of two hydrogen atoms (H) and an oxygen (O) atom. The molecule has an unequal distribution of charge on its surface, a quality known as polarity. The hydrogen atoms are slightly positively charged, while the oxygen atoms are slightly negatively charged. (B) The slightly positive regions of the water molecule are attracted to the slightly negative regions. This weak electrostatic attraction is a hydrogen bond. Hydrogen bonds exert a profound influence on the physical and chemical properties of water.

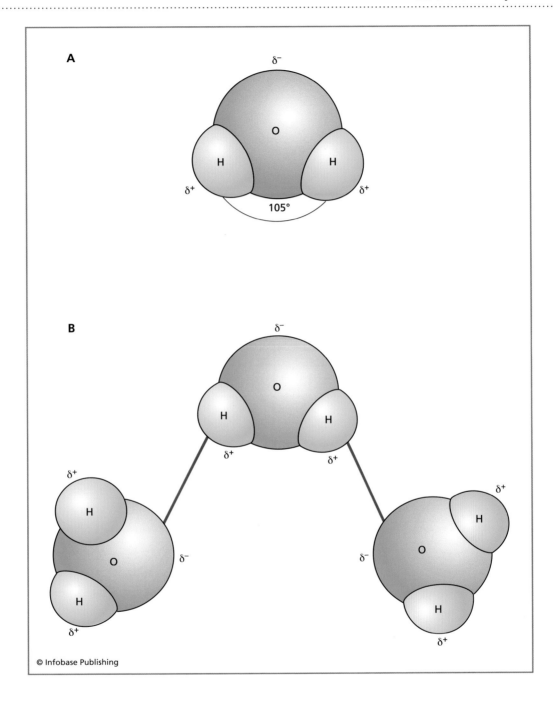

A

B

© Infobase Publishing

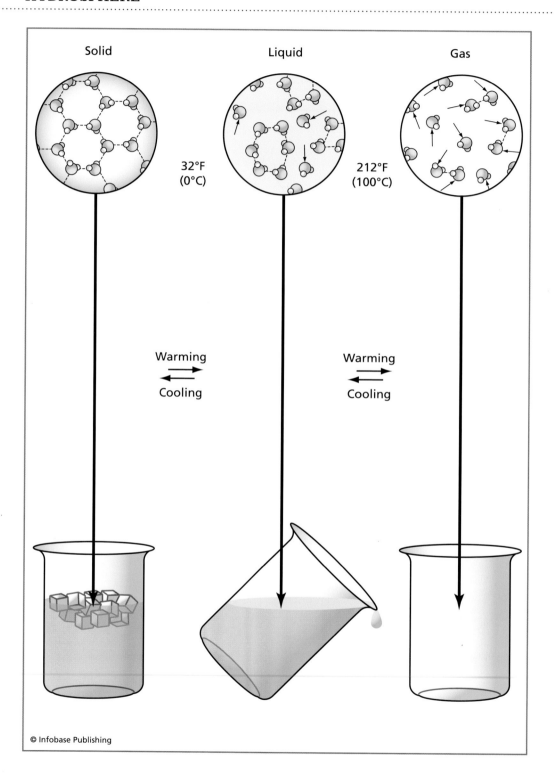

means that solid ice is less dense than very cold liquid water, in which hydrogen bonds hold the molecules together in small chains that pack closely together. In fact, water is densest just above freezing, at 39°F (4°C): It is the only substance that is denser as a liquid than as a solid. It is frigid liquid water—not solid ice—that sinks to the bottom of a pond when the weather gets cold. This is extremely important because it means that lakes in cold climates do not freeze solid in winter, which would prevent fish and other creatures from surviving. Hydrogen bonds also hold liquid water molecules weakly together at a pond's surface. The bound water molecules form a fragile elastic membrane that small insects can walk on.

Water's polarity makes it a great solvent. Solids, liquids, and gases dissolve better in water than in any other common liquid. If a salt crystal (usually sodium chloride [NaCl]) composed of positively charged sodium ions and negatively charged chlorine ions is immersed in freshwater, the salt dissolves. The positive sides of the water molecules are attracted to the chlorine ions of the salt crystal and surround them. Similarly, the negative sides of the water molecules surround the sodium ions. Unless the water evaporates, the ions cannot rejoin to form the original substance, and the salt remains dissolved in the water.

THE HYDROLOGIC CYCLE

Water moves continually between the Earth's water reservoirs: the oceans, atmosphere, terrestrial water features, and organisms. This cycling between reservoirs is known as the **hydrologic cycle** or water cycle.

Because of their huge size, the oceans play a major role in the water cycle. The Sun's rays evaporate water from the sea surface, creating water vapor, which may stay in the atmosphere for days or weeks.

On Earth, water is unique in existing in all three physical states—solid, liquid, and gas. In the solid state, water molecules are held together in a crystalline lattice. In the liquid state, water molecules move about relatively freely. In the gaseous state, water molecules move freely and tend to distribute themselves randomly throughout any container into which they are placed.

Water vapor is invisible but often condenses into tiny liquid droplets to form clouds. The droplets can come together to create **precipitation** in the form of rain, sleet, hail, snow, frost, or dew.

If the precipitation falls as snow, it may become frozen in a glacier or ice cap and remain there for hundreds or even thousands of years. When the ice melts, the water may join a stream that flows into a lake or pond. Precipitation that falls as rain may also join streams, lakes, and ponds. Some of this water will infiltrate soil and rock into a groundwater reservoir. Groundwater moves slowly through the rock beneath the Earth's surface but eventually emerges into a stream, a lake, or the ocean. Liquid water may evaporate into the sky—or may become part of a living organism—at any time. **Evapotranspiration** is the process of water evaporating from plants.

States of Matter

The same chemical substance can occur in three states—solid, liquid, or gas—each of which has a different structure. Molecules in solids are held in place by strong bonds; the molecules can vibrate within the structure. Solids have a definite size and shape, but they may bend or break if force is applied. Ice is the solid form of H_2O.

When heat is added to a solid, the molecules vibrate faster and farther apart. When a solid reaches its melting temperature, which is 32°F (0°C) for ice, the vibrations become more powerful than the bonds that hold the molecules together, and the molecules break free. Melting is the process that converts a solid to a liquid. Liquids have definite volume—they do not expand to take up more space, and they cannot be compressed—but they can flow to take the shape of their container.

With the addition of more heat, the molecules move more rapidly and apart by greater distances. When the substance reaches its boiling point, 212°F (100°C) for water, the molecules have enough energy to break entirely free of each other. The change in state from liquid to gas is known as **evaporation**. The floating molecules are now a gas; water vapor is the gaseous form of H_2O. Gases have neither size nor shape, although the molecules can collide with each other or with their container. **Condensation** is the opposite of evaporation, occurring when a gas cools enough to become a liquid.

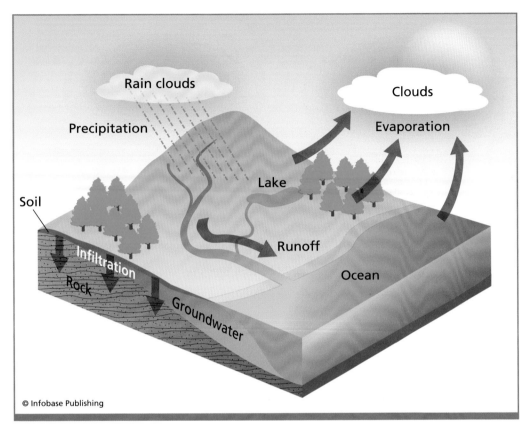

The Water Cycle. Water moves constantly between the Earth's reservoirs: bodies of water, the atmosphere, and living organisms.

WRAP-UP

Earth is unique in the solar system as the only planet with abundant water. Water travels between oceans, the atmosphere, glaciers, streams, ponds, and the ground in a continuous cycle. The structure of the water molecule gives water its unique properties. Hydrogen bonds keep ponds and lakes from freezing solid when it is cold, allowing fish and other creatures to survive during winter. Hydrogen bonds also allow lightweight insects to land on a pond's surface. Solids, liquids, and gases dissolve easily into water, which makes conditions right for life.

Surface Waters

As part of the hydrologic cycle, water flows through the oceans, evaporates into the atmosphere, rains down onto the land, and is absorbed by living organisms. Freshwater on land takes the form of solid ice in glaciers and ice caps and is a liquid in streams, ponds, lakes, and **wetlands**, which are the focus of this chapter. Streams linking these water reservoirs run from glaciers to ponds, from groundwater to lakes, and from lakes to the oceans. Lakes vary in most characteristics such as nutrient and gas content, water motions, and the **ecosystem**, for example. (An ecosystem includes the plants and animals of a region and the resources they need in order to live.)

Wetlands are poorly drained regions that are covered with fresh or saline water all or part of the time. They contain distinctive ecosystems, as do streams and lakes. Together, lakes, streams, and wetlands have provided food for people throughout history. Many inland people have long depended on freshwater fisheries for animal protein. In today's world, thanks to transportation improvements, ocean fish are easily available in developed countries, so much so that freshwater fish currently account for only about 5% of the global fish catch. In developed countries, much of the fishing in inland waters is recreational, although commercial fishing does take place in these areas in both developed and developing nations. Freshwater fish are being raised on farms in increasing numbers by a process called **aquaculture**. Aquaculture of both marine and freshwater fish is rapidly increasing, particularly in Asia.

GLACIERS

Glaciers store a tremendous amount of freshwater in the form of ice. Most of the snow that falls in the winter melts during the following spring or summer; but in cold climates, the winter snow may not melt at all. When the air is very cold, this snow becomes compressed by the weight of the new snow that falls on top of it; the deeper snow crystals become rounder and denser until they finally convert to ice. If the ice has not melted by the following winter, new snow falls on top of it. This accumulation of ice over the years creates a glacier. Glaciers grow when the amount of snow falling in winter exceeds the amount that melts in spring and summer and shrink when annual snowmelt exceeds snowfall.

Continental glaciers, also called ice caps, cover enormous areas of 20,000 square miles (50,000 square kilometers) or more. The ice cap spreads outward from the center, pushed by its own weight. The Antarctic and Greenland ice sheets, the only two ice caps currently on the Earth, hold 99% of the world's ice and about 75% of its freshwater. The largest of them, the Antarctic ice sheet, covers about 5 million square miles (13 million sq. km), nearly 1.5 times the size of the United States. The Greenland ice sheet covers 700,000 square miles (1.8 million sq. km) and reaches a thickness of more than 1.6 miles (2.7 km) in places.

Alpine glaciers grow in mountainous regions where winter snows are heavy and summers are short and cool. The glaciers flow downhill from their source in the mountains, where excess snow accumulates. The Siachen glacier in the Himalaya Mountains, at 48 miles (78 km) long, is the largest alpine glacier in the world. Its ice eventually melts to become the Indus River, which is a crucial source of water for both India and Pakistan.

The more water that glaciers trap as ice, the lower the overall sea level becomes. During ice ages, the sea level drops; but when glaciers and ice caps melt, it rises. Since the end of the Pleistocene ice age, around 10,000 years ago, the glaciers have been melting while the sea level has been rising.

STREAMS

Water flows in streams on the land surface between glaciers, lakes, ponds, groundwater, and the ocean. Wherever rain falls and snow melts, water drops collect as rivulets and run downhill into small channels. The location where a stream begins is called its **headwaters**. Headwaters usually begin in the mountains, where rain and snow are more abundant. Several small streams, known as **tributaries**, meet to form a river. A stream may also be fed by a **spring**, which is water that flows onto the surface from beneath the ground. A stream that flows year round is called **perennial**. For a perennial stream to flow when there is no rain or snowmelt, it must be fed by groundwater. An **ephemeral stream** flows only part of the year, usually during the rainy season.

Some perennial streams flow through deserts where there is little or no rain. For example, the Colorado River originates high in the Rocky Mountains of Colorado, where it is fed year round by snowmelt, rain, and groundwater. The fifth longest river in the United States, the Colorado rolls across the parched lands of Utah and Arizona and into Mexico, where evaporation far exceeds precipitation. The river currently provides water to rapidly growing desert cities such as Los Angeles, California; Las Vegas, Nevada; and Phoenix and Tucson in Arizona.

As the water flows, it picks up salts (present in such low concentrations that people do not taste them) and particles of dirt and organic matter such as tiny bits of leaves, dead animal tissue, and many other items. Large streams carry larger items such as sticks, leaves, animal waste, logs, brush, sand, pebbles, and even boulders. Some streams differ dramatically in such characteristics as temperature and sediment content along their lengths. For example, the same drop of water may enter a stream as melt water from a frigid, lifeless glacier and travel downstream for weeks until it becomes part of a warm, slow, sediment-filled river.

A river and all of its tributaries make up a **drainage basin** or **watershed.** North America's largest river basin, the Mississippi, drains 41% of the contiguous United States, or most of the area between the Rocky Mountains and the Appalachian Mountains. The Mississippi basin is the third largest river basin in the world, after the Amazon of

Havasu Falls, Grand Canyon, Arizona, is part of the water cycle. *(© Carmel Studios / SuperStock)*

South America and the Congo of Africa. The Mississippi River is the world's third longest river, after the Nile River of eastern Africa and the Amazon of South America. The Missouri River flows into the Mississippi; combined, these two rivers create the longest river in North America, a total of 3,895 miles (6,270 km). (Without the Missouri, the Mississippi is only the fourteenth longest river in the world.) On its journey into the Gulf of Mexico, the Mississippi runs through or borders 10 states: Minnesota, Wisconsin, Iowa, Illinois, Missouri, Kentucky, Arkansas, Tennessee, Mississippi, and Louisiana.

Drainage basins are separated by rock ridges known as **divides.** On either side of a **continental divide,** the water flows toward different oceans. For example, the crest of the Rocky Mountains forms

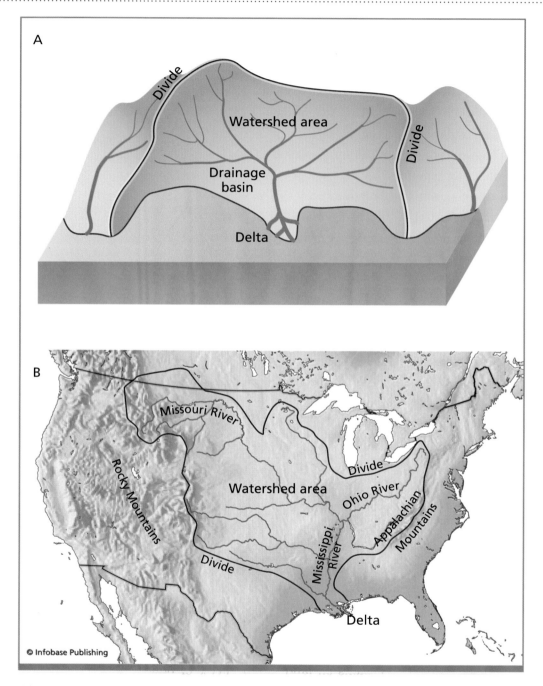

(A) A topographical depiction of a watershed. (B) A map illustrating the Mississippi watershed.

the continental divide in North America. Rain and snow falling on the east side of the divide drains into the Atlantic Ocean; precipitation on the west side drains into the Pacific Ocean.

Flooding

Streams vary greatly in size. The amount of water they carry changes by season and by year. When more water flows down a stream than its channel can hold, or when a natural lake or **reservoir** (an artificial lake) overflows its banks or a dam, flooding occurs. Floods are caused by heavy rain, rapid snow melt, or surge from storms coming in from the ocean (such as during a hurricane). Summer thunderstorms that drop copious amounts of rain may initiate sudden torrents of water and mud called **flash floods** that race through mountain valleys or desert canyons. In flatter regions, floodwaters overflow a stream's banks onto the nearby flatlands (which are called **floodplains**).

Floods are important because they enrich floodplain soil with nutrients that are important to ecosystems. Throughout human history, farmers have depended on regular spring floods for the soil fertility they need to grow their crops. Many animal and plant species are adapted to flood conditions, and some even need floods as part of their life cycle. For example, cottonwood trees need floodwaters to germinate. Many insects wait for flooding to lay their eggs, hatch, or metamorphose. Floods also flush dead plants into streams, providing food for fish and other organisms. For some fish species, spring floods become the trigger to breed. Waterfowl depend on the wetlands created by floods for their habitat. Floods also wash dead trees and brush into streams, providing habitat for animals such as the beaver (*Castor canadensis*).

LAKES AND PONDS

Water collects in depressions on land to form lakes or ponds. Water may stay in these reservoirs, briefly or for years, until it evaporates or flows into another reservoir. Lakes vary both horizontally and vertically

Satellite image of the Great Lakes (NASA). The lakes comprise 20% of the world's surface freshwater. *(NASA)*

in features such as light levels, temperature, and water contents. Different lakes also have distinctive features.

The majority of natural lakes in the United States are found in four areas: the Great Lakes region, the Adirondack Mountains of the Northeast, the Pacific Northwest, and Florida. Collectively, the Great Lakes form the largest freshwater body in the world, accounting for 20% of the world's surface freshwater. All five of the Great Lakes are in the top 15 largest lakes in the world. The Great Lakes region and the Adirondacks were glaciated during the Pleistocene epoch, and the depressions left in the bedrock by the retreating glaciers later filled with water. Glaciers also leave blocks of ice in glacial **sediment** (broken up rocks and dirt); that ice later melts to create kettle lakes. These small lakes dot the landscape in Minnesota (which is nicknamed "The Land of 10,000 Lakes") and other locations in the northern United States and southern Canada.

Lakes can form without glaciation. In mountain ranges such as those in the Pacific Northwest, melting glaciers and snow supply water for lakes. Water can fill a volcanic crater or caldera, as it has at Crater Lake, Oregon. Water also dissolves rock limestone to create depressions that fill with water, such as in the Florida Everglades. A stream that winds its way across the landscape may cut off a meander, or loop, to form an oxbow lake. Lakes can also arise in swampy regions where groundwater floods the surface. The world's deepest (5,712 feet [2,741 meters]) and most voluminous freshwater lake is Lake Baikal, in Siberia. This lake fills an active earthquake fault that deepens when the land along the fault moves.

Lakes have a life cycle. Over time, they fill with sediment, until they become **swamps**, meadows, and, eventually, even forests. Lakes, present and former, in all of these stages, can be seen today. In geologic terms, lakes are short lived, existing only in the millennia after glacial periods. Because the Pleistocene epoch ended only 10,000 years ago—relatively recently in geologic time—an unusual number of lakes exist today.

Beautiful, blue Crater Lake is the centerpiece of Crater Lake National Park, Oregon, and fills a volcanic caldera. *(© Joe Sohm / The Image Works)*

Light is greatest at a lake's surface and decreases with depth; it can penetrate to a greater depth in clear water than in murky water. In shallow lakes, light may penetrate to the bottom; but deep lakes become dark at middle and deep levels. Where light reaches, the process called **photosynthesis** can occur. Here, plants absorb carbon dioxide (CO_2) and water to create sugar ($C_6H_{12}O_6$) for food energy, and oxygen (O_2) in the presence of sunlight. The simplified chemical reaction for photosynthesis is:

$$6CO_2 + 12H_2O + \text{solar energy} = C_6H_{12}O_6 + 6O_2 + 6H_2O$$

Because this process requires sunlight, photosynthesis takes place at or near a lake's surface. Aquatic photosynthesizers include grasses and other plants that have their roots anchored to the bottom of the lake and **phytoplankton**, which are tiny algae that float at or near the lake's surface.

Different lakes contain different kinds of salts, dissolved gases, acidity, and nutrients. Lakes turn saline when so little water flows from the lake that most of the water lost is lost by evaporation. The water flowing into a lake contains minute quantities of salt. When water flows out, the salts go with it. But when water evaporates, the salts stay behind. Saline lakes are found in arid regions, where evaporation exceeds precipitation and outflow. For example, the Great Salt Lake in Utah is nearly eight times as salty as the ocean.

Lakes contain dissolved gases, the most important of which are carbon dioxide and oxygen. Cold water holds more gases than warm water; if water is warmed, the gases bubble out. Gases enter the water primarily from the air at the lake's surface. Dissolved carbon dioxide (CO_2) is used by plants for photosynthesis. Carbon dioxide breaks apart water; this increases the amount of hydrogen ions (H^+) in the water and forms carbonic acid.

Fish and other aquatic life breathe oxygen that has dissolved in the water at the lake surface or that has been formed as a byproduct of photosynthesis. More creatures live near the lake shore, but they can

Acidity and pH

Acidity is an important feature of water chemistry. When H_2O breaks apart, it forms hydrogen ions (H^+) and hydroxyl ions (OH^-). In pure water, the amount of H^+ equals the amount of OH^-. If a substance added to water brings about an excess of H^+, the solution becomes an **acid**. If OH^- is in excess, the solution is **alkaline**.

Acidity and alkalinity are measured on the **pH** scale with numbers from 0 to 14. The H in pH refers to the quantity of free, positively charged hydrogen ions. Pure

(continues)

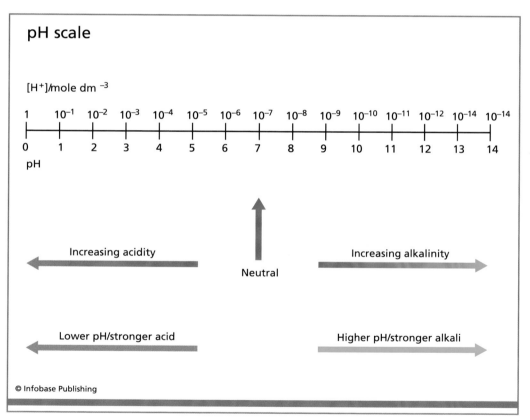

pH scale

$[H^+]$/mole dm^{-3}

| 1 | 10^{-1} | 10^{-2} | 10^{-3} | 10^{-4} | 10^{-5} | 10^{-6} | 10^{-7} | 10^{-8} | 10^{-9} | 10^{-10} | 10^{-11} | 10^{-12} | 10^{-14} | 10^{-14} |

pH: 0 1 2 3 4 5 6 7 8 9 10 11 12 13 14

Increasing acidity ← → Increasing alkalinity

Neutral

Lower pH/stronger acid ← → Higher pH/stronger alkali

© Infobase Publishing

The pH scale. A neutral solution has a pH of 7.0; less than 7.0 is acidic, and greater than 7.0 is alkaline. Hydrogen ion concentration is shown on the upper axis of the scale.

(continues)
water is neutral, with a pH of 7. Solutions with pH lower than 7 are acidic; those with the lowest pH are the strongest acids. Acidic substances, such as lemons, have a sour taste. Strong acids can burn skin and other tissue. Numbers higher than 7 are alkaline (also called basic); the highest pH numbers are the strongest bases. Strong bases, such as lye, can also harm tissue.

The pH scale is logarithmic, so a change in one unit reflects a tenfold change in acidity. If clean rain has a pH of 5.6, rain with a pH of 4.6 is ten times more acidic and a pH of 3.6 is 100 times more acidic.

be found even in the open water and in deep areas. In winter, when ice coats a lake, plants cannot photosynthesize, and new oxygen cannot enter the water from the air; thus, organisms must survive on the oxygen that is already there.

Nutrients are ions that are essential to plants and animals. They include elements that are critical to plant cell growth, such as nitrogen and phosphorus. Other elements, such as silica and calcium, are in shells and skeletons, while nitrates and phosphates are components of proteins and other compounds. Nutrients are also needed for photosynthesis. Nutrient ions come from the atmosphere, or from leaves and other living matter that fall into the lakes and rivers.

When aquatic plants and animals die, their tissues and the nutrients they contain sink slowly to the bottom of the lake. If the lake is deep, the nutrients fall into the dark depths where no plants can live and make use of them. Lakes such as these, called **oligotrophic**, have few usable nutrients and so can support little plant life. Brilliant blue Crater Lake, Oregon, is classified as an ultra-oligotrophic lake. Lake Tahoe, on the California–Nevada border, is oligotrophic but is losing clarity due to development in its watershed.

In a shallow lake, nutrients also fall to the bottom but because sunlight can reach them, plants can use the nutrients for photosynthesis. The abundant plant life of a shallow lake gives it a green hue.

These lakes may also be covered with a green scum of plants and phytoplankton. **Bacteria** thrive in these **eutrophic** lakes. Bacteria are microscopic, single-celled organisms that are not plants or animals but are members of their own kingdom. These tiny organisms decompose organic material and use oxygen as plants and animals do. However, eutrophic lakes are often oxygen poor.

Before Europeans arrived, the Great Lakes were mainly oligotrophic due to their size and depth. They had few plant nutrients, but still enough to support abundant animal life. However, as agriculture and urbanization have increased in the watersheds, nutrients from human sources have enriched the lakes. The shallowest lake, Lake Erie, is now eutrophic, and most of the others are mesotrophic lakes, a level between the two categories. Lake Superior, the largest and deepest of them, contains enough water so that it still is oligotrophic.

Besides light, sunshine brings heat to a lake. Lakes in summer are vertically stratified; that is, sunshine heats the lake's upper layer so that the surface water is warmer than the deeper water. Warm water is less dense than cool water, so the warm water remains on top, where it absorbs gases from the atmosphere. Life is abundant in the surface water layer, where the light and gases allow photosynthesis. The lake's lower layer receives less light and has no contact with the atmosphere. If bacteria in these waters consume the available oxygen, the deep layer becomes oxygen poor, or **anoxic** (without oxygen).

When temperatures decrease in the autumn, surface water becomes cooler and denser and sinks, causing the deeper water to rise. This autumn **turnover** brings dissolved oxygen into the deeper waters, which allows fish and other animals to live there. Where winters are cold, low temperatures freeze the lake's surface, which turns to ice; the ice is less dense than the frigid water below. Fish swim in the waters beneath the ice, where they live on nutrients and dissolved gases found there. In spring, when the ice layer melts, that frigid water becomes denser than the water beneath it and sinks toward the bottom, and the lake water turns over again.

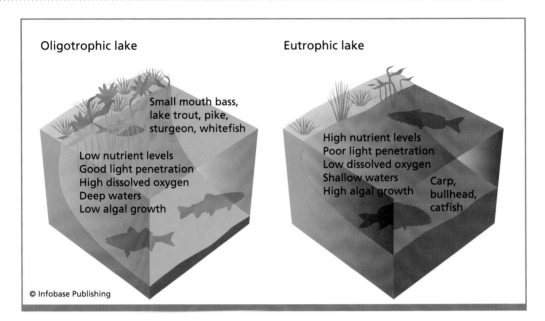

Features of an oligotrophic lake and a eutrophic lake.

Temperatures in shallow lakes do not vary enough to allow stratification. If the water is too shallow for turnover to occur, organisms living below the surface use up the oxygen and cause the bottom water to become anoxic. Eventually, nothing but anoxic bacteria resides in the lower portions of the lake.

Like the oceans, large lakes have currents and waves. Lake currents form when water with different characteristics—for example, river water, rainwater, or groundwater—is added. Wind can also generate surface water currents. In Lake Michigan, one of the Great Lakes, winds push the surface water to the northeast, where it piles up on the shore. When the "hill" created by the piling becomes too high, the water plunges beneath the surface and forms a current that flows back to the southwest side of the lake. Lake surface winds also form waves. Wave size depends on the wind's strength and the distance it travels over the surface. Larger lakes are capable of hosting larger waves.

Tides, the motions of water due to the gravitational pull of the Moon and Sun on the Earth, occur in lakes, but they are mostly

Sparks Lake, in Deschutes National Forest, Oregon, is laden with plant life and naturally eutrophic. *(© age fotostock / SuperStock)*

swamped out by the lake's **seiche**. Seiches are internal waves that cause water to move up and down in a sloshing motion around the basin. Each lake's seiche has its own period, which is the amount of time it takes for the crest of a wave to pass the same point on the lakeshore. The seiche period of a small lake, such as Lach Treig in Scotland, is short, at only 9 minutes. The seiche period of Lake Erie is a long 880 minutes.

FRESHWATER ECOSYSTEMS

Streams, lakes, and other freshwater bodies support rich and complex ecosystems. An estimated 12% of all animal species live in freshwater ecosystems, and most other terrestrial species depend in some way on freshwater ecosystems for their survival.

A **food web** is the complex network of feeding relationships among the organisms in an ecosystem. Supporting the base of an aquatic food web are photosynthesizing phytoplankton and plants. Organisms that cannot make their own food must eat other plants or animals. The tiniest of these organisms are **zooplankton**, which range in size from 0.04 to 0.12 inches (1 to 3 millimeters) and feed on phytoplankton. Soft-bodied **invertebrates**—animals without backbones—may have a hard outer covering, such as a shell, for protection. These animals have many eating strategies: Some, such as worms or snails, tunnel through or slide along lake mud, eating organic material; others, such as freshwater mussels, may filter their food right from the water. If the **sediment** contains a large amount of organic material, invertebrate life will be abundant and diverse.

Further up the food web, small fish species feed on zooplankton, bacteria, or decaying plant and animal tissue; above them, larger fish consume the small fish. Finally, ducks and other waterfowl, plus beavers and other mammals, feed on the fish or invertebrates below them on the food web.

Completing the food web are **decomposers**, which are usually bacteria. Decomposers break down dead plant and animal tissue and animal wastes into nutrients that can be used by plants or animals. Without decomposers to recycle nutrients, life on Earth could not exist.

In the shallows near a lake's shore, where sunlight can penetrate to the bottom, aquatic plants live with their roots at the bottom and leaves near the surface and provide food and habitat for animals. In a eutrophic lake, green scum coating the surface is filled with phytoplankton, bacteria, fungi, and other organisms that feed on dead or decaying organic material. In an oligotrophic lake, sunlight penetrates deeply, allowing photosynthesis to take place even in deep waters. For example, algae in Lake Tahoe grew at depths of up to 330 feet (100 m) before **pollutants** obscured the lake's clarity.

The **riparian corridor** is a ribbon of vegetation that thrives along the banks of streams. Here, the stream provides water, nutrients, and organic materials that allow plants to grow that are different from those that grow in areas farther away from the stream bank. A perennial stream running through an arid region, for example, supports leafy trees and an abundance of plants that are not found in the nearby desert. As streams flow through the riparian corridor, they receive organic material, such as leaves and dead bugs. Streams also help living things such as plants, fungi, larvae, crustaceans, mollusks, worms, fishes, and mammals to migrate to new habitats.

WETLANDS

Extremely biologically productive areas, wetlands are homes to varied and complex ecosystems. The three types of wetlands—marshes, swamps, and bogs—are defined by the soil and plant types found within them.

Marshes are the most common and widespread wetlands in the United States. Their water may be tidal (saline) or fresh, and may come from surface or groundwater sources. The rich soils and nearly neutral pH of marshes provide the foundation for one of the richest ecosystems on Earth. Soft-stemmed plants such as water lilies, cattails, reeds, and bulrushes and a wide variety of wildlife make their home in marshes. These ecosystems teem with waterfowl and mammals such as otters (*Lutra* sp.) and muskrats (*Ondata zibethicus*). The Florida Everglades are a spectacular example of a marsh ecosystem.

Swamps form in poorly drained depressions where hardwood trees and other woody plants thrive. Swamp flora in temperate climates, such as in the northeastern United States, includes sphagnum moss (*Sphagnum fimbriatum*), the red maple, (*Acer rubrum*), and various rushes and grasses. Cypress and mangrove forests dominate tropical areas. Swamp vegetation provides great habitat for invertebrates such as freshwater shrimp, crayfish, and clams and for fish, water birds, and such small mammals as beavers and otters. Rare species, such as the American crocodile, are also found in swamps. Approximately 100,000 square miles (260,000 sq. km) of the United States, particularly in the Atlantic and Gulf Coast states, are covered with swamps, although many square miles of swamp have been lost in recent decades. For example, draining and development have reduced the Great Dismal Swamp of southeastern Virginia to less than half its original size.

Bogs are small lakes that have no inlet or outlet in the form of streams or rivers. Their water comes from rainfall. With no inflow, bog soils have fewer nutrients and are more acidic than other wetlands. Bogs are covered with spongy **peat**, which is partially decomposed organic matter formed by layers of dead plants and covered by a thick cover of sphagnum moss. Over time, other plants and animals, including the carnivorous sundew (*Drosera* sp.), will move into such an area. Most bogs in the United States are found in old lakes in the formerly glaciated areas of the northeastern and Great Lakes regions, where tall cotton grass (*Eriophorum angustifolium*), cranberry (*Vaccinium macrocarpon*), blueberry (*Vaccinium* sp.), tamarack (*Larix laricina*), and various pines grow. These plants support animals such as moose (*Alces alces*), lynx (*Lynx canadensis*), and various deer. Evergreen trees and shrubs grow in southeastern bogs, where black bears roam. Bogs are sometimes drained for farmland, and their rich peat deposits are used for fuel.

Great egrets in the morning fog in the Florida Everglades. *(© Fritz Polking / The Image Works)*

FRESHWATER FISHERIES

Surface water sources are home to many food sources, especially fish. Freshwater fishing takes place in lakes, streams, and wetlands, and in manmade reservoirs and ponds. Inland fisheries contribute about 12% of all fish consumed by humans. Well-known freshwater fish include various trout, catfish, tilapia (*Tilapia* sp.), lake whitefish (*Coregonus clupeaformis*), and carp (*Cyprinus carpio*). Important food species also include salmon, Atlantic whitefish (*Coregonus huntsmani*), and sturgeon (*Acipenser* sp.), which live in the sea but spawn in freshwater, while fish such as the American eel (*Anguilla rostrata*) spawn in the sea but live in freshwater.

Inland waters have enormous variations in their **primary productivity** (the amount of food energy created). The type and abundance of lake fish are determined by characteristics such as the quantity of nutrients and dissolved oxygen. Fish species may also vary along a single stream's course: Trout can be caught in a river's cold, clean headwaters, while smelt and flounder thrive far downstream in the warmer, brackish estuary.

Much of the fishing that takes place today in inland waters is recreational, and important to many local economies. Lakes and streams are often stocked with fry, or small fish, that are allowed to grow to a size large enough for recreational fishers, who may also practice "catch and release," meaning that the fish are released back into the water after they are caught. Great Lakes recreational fishing brings in about $4.5 billion annually from species such as Lake Whitefish (*Coregonus clupeaformi*), chub, and yellow perch (*Perca flavescens*). Although any water can be fished recreationally, only large lakes and rivers are fished commercially. Three factors have hurt commercial fishing in inland waters in recent years: competition from recreational fishing, overfishing, and pollution. Competition with recreational fishers is decreasing the scope of some commercial fishing. Commercial fishing of walleye (*Stizostedion vitreum*), for example, is banned to preserve fish populations for sports fishing.

Overfishing occurs where there are not enough mature fish left to replenish those that have been caught. In developed nations, some freshwater fisheries that were extensively overfished in the past are recovering. Despite these efforts, however, fish such as the lake sturgeon of the Great Lakes remain critically endangered. In addition, developing nations are not managing their inland fisheries well. Many large freshwater fish in the Mekong River of Southeast Asia, including what is considered the world's largest freshwater fish, the Mekong giant catfish (*Pangasianodon gigas*), are endangered. Fisheries are being exploited systematically, with the largest fish being fished out first, followed by the removal of progressively smaller species, until nothing is left.

Freshwater fisheries in the United States have been in decline because of pollution for several decades. **Water pollution** is a change in the chemical, physical, and biological health of a waterway due to

The Florida Everglades

The most magnificent wetlands in the United States are the Florida Everglades, extending across 4,000 square miles (10,000 sq. km) of southern Florida. The Everglades lie in a shallow limestone basin where water flows across in sheets. Islands of intertwined trees and shrubs, such as palms, pines, live oaks, cypresses, and other tropical species, punctuate grassy plains. A wealth of birds, particularly large wading birds such as the roseate spoonbill

(continues)

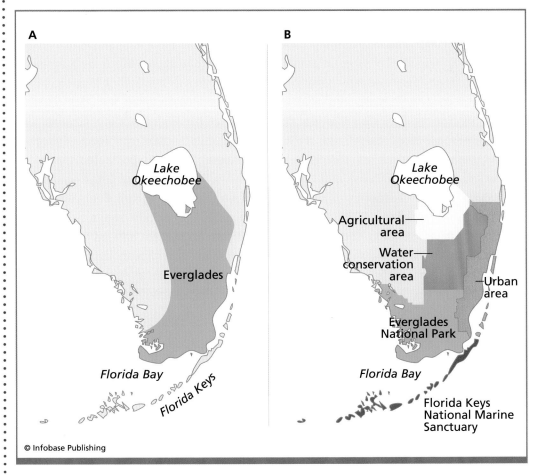

© Infobase Publishing

The extent of the Florida Everglades before the arrival of Europeans *(left)* and today.

(continues)

(Ajaia ajaja), wood stork (*Mycteria americana*), great blue heron (*Ardea herodias*), white ibis (*Eudocimus albus*), and various egrets, live among alligators (*Alligator mississippiensis*) and several types of snakes and turtles. The tree islands shelter many reptiles, such as the coral snake (*Micrurus fulvius fulvius*), the eastern indigo snake (*Drymarchon corais couperi*), the king snake (*Lampropeltis getula*), and the red rat snake (*Elaphe guttata guttata*). The islands also shelter larger mammals, such as deer (*Cervidae* sp.) and black bears (*Ursus americanus*), and wildcats, including the endangered Florida panther (*Felis concolor coryi*), as well as small mammals, such as the gray fox (*Urocyon cinereoargenteus*) and raccoon (*Procyon lotor*). Crocodiles (*Crocodylus acutus*) and manatees (*Trichechus manatus latirostrisi*) roam the near-shore saltwater regions. These wetlands receive more than 60 inches (152 centimeters) of rain annually.

European settlers initially hunted the birds of the Everglades for their feather plumes and alligators for their skins. Later, when swamp soils were found to have high organic content, the marshes were drained for farming. Vegetable and cattle farming now take up about one-fifth of the original area of the Everglades. In addition to land development, flood control and roads (especially the Tamiami Trail, which is a continuation of U.S. Highway 41) have disrupted the 60-mile (100-km) "River of Grass" that once flowed west across the Everglades to the Gulf of Mexico.

Draining swamps has destroyed the habitat for many wildlife species. Since its establishment in 1947, Everglades National Park has protected the habitat, plants, and animals of 2,354 square miles (6,097 sq. km) of the Everglades. Since 1994, public concern about the loss of this diverse ecosystem has led to the creation of projects designed to "replumb" the Everglades, such as removing levees and reflooding drained swampland.

human activity. Because of it, many species have been restricted or banned entirely for human consumption. For example, several fisheries in the Great Lakes, including walleye and channel catfish fisheries, were closed in 1970 due to mercury contamination. While most of the fisheries reopened 10 years later, the walleye fishery remains closed. **Invasive** or **alien species**, introduced by human activities into locations where they are not native, have taken a large toll on some native fish populations.

Developing countries are also experiencing a decline in fish production. The combination of dams, deforestation, and the conversion of 400 square miles (1,000 sq. km) of mangrove swamps to rice paddies and fish ponds, for example, has dropped overall fish production on the Mekong River of Southeast Asia by two thirds.

FRESHWATER AQUACULTURE

Expanding populations and changing diet are fueling a global rise in demand for fish. To fill the need, fish and shellfish are increasingly grown in the same way people raise animals—on farms. Worldwide, aquaculture is a $50-billion-a-year industry and could account for more than half of all fish production by 2030. Although aquaculture is rapidly increasing in the oceans, more than half of farmed fish comes from fresh water.

Most farmed fish are sold for food, but freshwater species also supply fish for aquariums and fish and bait for sport and commercial fishing. Commercial aquaculture in prosperous nations focuses on high-priced items such as shrimp, crayfish, prawns, trout, salmon, and oysters. Production of catfish, carp, and tilapia is also increasing. Catfish farming in the United States has increased five-fold since the 1960s.

Like farm animals on land, farmed fish must be raised in a safe and healthy environment. They must reproduce easily in captivity, be inexpensive to feed, and be able to survive in an enclosed environment. Fish can be farmed in earthen or concrete ponds, behind barricades, or in cages suspended in the water. Where fish population density is high, keeping them healthy and their wastes flushed out are big priorities.

Carp are raised using similar techniques around the world. Their spawning ponds are kept shallow and warm. After spawning, the parent fish are removed from the pond. After the fry hatch, they are moved to nursing ponds, which are rich in plankton. The following year, the small fish are placed in larger ponds; in Asia, they are often moved to rice fields. Pond-raised carp are fed plant materials such as soybean meal and rice bran, which are inexpensive and have a smaller environmental impact than feeds made from other fish.

Trout are popular for both sport fishing and as a food. Farmed trout need good water circulation and are often raised in the cold and pure water found in mountainous regions. Trout hatcheries use artificial fertilization and keep the eggs separate from older fish, while young fry are placed in small ponds for feeding. Because trout are meat eaters, they are often fed meatpacking byproducts.

WRAP-UP

Surface waters cycle through glaciers, streams, lakes and ponds, and wetlands. Melting glaciers feed some of the world's major rivers, which carry water and nutrients downstream. River floods enable some plants and animals to complete their life cycles, enrich the soils, and create habitat. Lakes vary greatly in temperature, nutrient content, and other factors, but many of them have thriving ecosystems. Wetlands contain magnificent ecosystems and provide many services to life on Earth. Surface water ecosystems have long been a food source for the people who live nearby. With careful management, these fisheries should continue to provide a source of food and jobs to inland communities in the future, as well. Aquaculture will continue to grow as a source of fish for the future.

Surface Water Resources

Besides being a source of freshwater fish and other foods, streams, lakes, and ponds—collectively called **waterways**—have many uses that will be discussed in this chapter. For example, most of the world's cities and towns are built on waterways. Waterways supply water for drinking and irrigation. They provide transportation for people and goods and serve as a source of cooling for machines used in industrial processes. Waterways also provide energy, food, and waste disposal for people and their developments. To use water resources on a large scale often requires the construction of extensive engineering projects, such as pumps, that supply water to communities. Projects such as dams provide year-round water storage, in addition to flood control, power, and recreational opportunities. In addition, levee construction protects communities from flooding. This chapter also covers how the engineering of waterways has a downside for people and the environment by keeping sediments from replenishing the soil and wetlands. Dam projects can change water conditions that cause the loss of native fish species along with the submerging of important environmental and cultural resources.

USE OF SURFACE WATER

Water has a variety of uses, and these uses differ in developed and developing countries. In both instances, water is primarily used for agriculture—irrigated agriculture supplies about 40% of the world's food crops. Agriculture accounts for 41% of freshwater use in the United States and 70% of global usage. Domestic uses, such as drinking and bathing, consume only a relatively small amount, about 10% in both the United States and globally. Industry and power-plant cooling takes up the rest: Industry uses 11% of the water in the United States and 20% globally; power-plant cooling water accounts for 38% of U.S. water use, but a very small amount in the rest of the world.

In areas with wet climates, streams run continually, and water is widely available. However, this is not true in deserts, where there is little rain and no snowmelt for water for drinking or irrigation. In these harsh environments, large perennial rivers, such as the Colorado River in the southwestern United States, are essential for establishing stable desert communities.

Waterways provide easy and cheap transportation for goods and people. Since prehistoric times, waterways have been at the center of trade networks in wetter climates. Even now, about one-sixth of the intercity freight of the United States, totaling billions of dollars, is shipped up and down the Mississippi River and its tributaries each year. These streams make up a 14,500-mile (23,300-km) system of inland waterways. The cost of river transport adds up to about one-half that of rails and one-tenth that of roadways.

Industry in the developed world has grown dependant on the large-scale use of water for manufacturing and for power generation. Production of a single car requires up to 29,000 gallons (110,000 liters) of water. The computer industry in the United States needs 475 billion gallons (1,800 billion l) a year.

Power-generating plants, such as coal or nuclear power plants, use water to create steam to produce electricity. Nationwide, these plants use billions of gallons of water daily to cool their turbines. A single large turbine in a coal-fired plant may use 3.5 to 5 million gallons (13 to 19 million l) of water per day. A nuclear power station can use 34 million gallons (130 million l) of ground water a day. Power plants must be built near large natural water bodies such as an ocean, sea, or major river. Other types of industrial plants use water for cooling as well.

USE OF WETLANDS

Wetlands provide enormous benefits to the environment and to society. These soggy lands reduce flood damage by absorbing water during floods. Water in wetlands seeps into the soil to refill groundwater supplies. Wetlands also provide water to streams, a function that is especially important during droughts. Many plants and animals depend on wetlands for food and habitat. Wetlands also serve as nurseries for young animals and as nesting sites for migratory waterfowl. The young of many commercially valuable species of edible fish and seafood get their start in wetlands. As water trickles through wetlands, the rich soil filters excess sediments, nutrients, and other pollutants. (Pollutants are substances that are found in unnatural quantities in an environment, or in a region of an environment where they do not belong. They may be substances that are manufactured by humans and do not belong in that environment at all.) The aquatic organisms that live in wetlands also degrade pollutants, so water that flows from a wetland is purer than when it entered.

The United States has a long history of destroying wetlands because of the failure to understand their important contributions, and the belief that these swamps exist in abundance. The federal Arkansas Act of 1850 and the Green Act of 1868 essentially directed the states to convert wetlands into ports, harbors, rail lines, roads, and agricultural and recreational lands, so for nearly two centuries, people in the

United States have plowed or paved over their swamps and sloughs. Wetlands converted to farmland have rich soils that are highly productive. Because wetlands are often situated near rivers or the coast, they are desirable locations for development, resulting in high land values. As a result, more than 80% of the wetlands in California and the midwestern states have been lost.

Although the U.S. Congress has acted to protect wetlands, loopholes in wetlands protection laws allow continued destruction. Wetlands are supposed to be developed only if all other possibilities are exhausted, and developers must replace the wetlands they destroy. But few development projects are ever turned down, and the replacement wetlands are often located far away from the original site or are of poor quality. The result is that enormous areas of wetlands are still being lost.

Wetlands loss has taken its toll. It is part of the reason that nearly two-thirds of California's native fish are extinct, endangered, threatened, or in decline. Forested wetlands near the Mississippi River once had the capacity to store about 60 days of river discharge, but their removal has now reduced storage capacity to about 12 days of discharge. Researchers say that the flooding of the Gulf of Mexico coast from Hurricane Katrina would have been much less extensive had the region not lost so many of its wetlands over the past century. Since the 1930s, Louisiana has lost more than 1,900 square miles (5,000 sq. km) of wetlands, an area as large as Delaware. Without wetlands, nutrients and other pollutants make their way more readily to streams, lakes, and oceans.

WATERWAYS AND THE RISE OF CIVILIZATIONS

Cities and civilizations are entirely dependent on the availability of water. Access to surface water is so important that, until recently, settlements could only thrive if they were built along a river or lake. Permanent settlements were made possible by canals, which divert river and lake water onto agricultural land. Some of the earliest permanent settlements began 10,000 years ago on the Jordan River, at Jericho in the Middle East. More than 6,000 years ago, areas along the Tigris-Euphrates and the Nile were settled. These communities evolved from hunting camps to farms and then to towns. The ability to live in a location year round led the rise of communities and cultures.

Rivers provide important communication between parts of a civilization. Rome, Italy, grew where an island in the center of the Tiber (Tevere) River made crossing the river relatively easy. From a small settlement of farmers and shepherds along the banks of the Tiber, a village grew as the crossing become part of the major north-south route through Italy. In time, the community blossomed into the metropolis of Rome, the center of the ancient civilization that would conquer and control all of Italy, southern Europe, the Middle East, and Egypt. By the start of the first century A.D., the Roman Empire had grown to be the most powerful and largest empire in the world.

Roman engineers brought water into the city via huge aqueducts from as far away as 60 miles (100 km). They built ports and shipped materials—including large amounts of building stone and foodstuffs such as wheat, oil, and wine—along the river. The Tiber served as Rome's naval base in the third century B.C. Although the Tiber was at the center of a flourishing trade network for centuries, the river is now too silted up to use for commerce, except within the city of Rome itself.

As the Romans conquered distant lands, rivers played an important role in the development of their empire. Seven years after the Romans successfully invaded Britain in A.D. 43, they built a wooden bridge over the Thames River, just east of where the London Bridge is today. The bridge became the focal point of the Roman road system through Britain, and it attracted traders and settlers. The city of London grew up around this bridge. Boats from up the river could bring materials into the city for the manufacturing of goods, which could be taken by ships down the river to the sea to be sold in distant lands. For centuries, the Thames served as a source of water for domestic and commercial use, transportation, and waste disposal. Now, however, commercial ships no longer travel the Thames, and the old docks have been converted to residential and commercial properties.

The incredibly well-preserved aqueduct at Pont du Gard, Provence, France, illustrates how the Romans transported water to their settlements. *(© age fotostock / SuperStock)*

After the Roman Empire fell, the Romans' extensive road system disintegrated, and rivers became the only easy method of travel and transport. Rivers also carried wastes away from the cities. For these reasons, thirteen of Western Europe's national capitals are located on large rivers. These capitals include Vienna, Austria; Budapest, Hungary; and Belgrade, Serbia and Montenegro—all located on the Danube—and Sofia, Bulgaria, and Bucharest, Romania, both located on Danube feeder streams. Paris, France, was founded more than 2,000 years ago on an island in the Seine River.

While traveling in new areas, explorers, traders, conquerors, and settlers used waterways to exploit and acquire lands. North American waterways supplied routes for European exploration, conquest, and settlement. Channels, or canals, were built to connect natural waterways, making travel easier. Major cities were built along one or more rivers to maximize travel to other areas. Pittsburgh, Pennsylvania, was founded at the juncture of three rivers: the Allegheny, the Monongahela, and the Ohio. St. Louis, Missouri, is at the juncture of the Missouri, Illinois, and Mississippi Rivers. The metropolitan area of Portland, Oregon, straddles the Willamette River. In addition, Portland and its sister city, Vancouver, Washington, are on opposite sides of the Columbia River.

New York City became the most economically and culturally important city in the United States in part because of its access to important waterways. The city and port are located where the Hudson River flows into New York Harbor. Its proximity to the Hudson makes New York City both the gateway to the North American continent and, through New York Harbor, a link to the world's oceans. The quality of the harbor and the access the river provided to the rest of the American continent led the Dutch West India Company to establish a small trading post on the southern tip of Manhattan Island in the early 1600s.

ENGINEERING A STREAM

The water in streams and lakes can be accessed without complicated engineering by direct pumping for use by a city, town, or agricultural area. However, engineering can foster more effective use of a body of water and can protect riverside communities that are vulnerable to flooding. But while engineering a stream protects communities and makes the water supply more dependable, it also decreases some of the river's benefits, such as the replacement of nutrients on the floodplain.

Engineers build a variety of structures, such as dams and levees, to control and use streams. Dams built across a riverbed block the flow of water, creating a reservoir on the upstream side. Reservoirs store water for use by homes and farms during the dry season, allowing people to dwell and farm in deserts and other formerly inhospitable regions. Besides providing a stable, year-round water supply, dams provide power and flood control. Boaters and fishers value reservoirs for their recreational opportunities.

There are several types of dams. Check dams prevent flooding in small areas, and diversion dams divert water to irrigate crops. Irrigation, much of it from diversion dams, helps to grow about 40% of the world's food. Flood control dams, constructed of concrete or huge mounds of rock, gravel, sand, and clay, catch floodwaters. In addition to being used for water storage and flood control, large concrete hydroelectric dams harness power.

Water rushing through a narrow opening or cascading down a rock face creates a tremendous amount of **kinetic energy**, the energy that comes from motion. The energy of falling water is called hydroelectric power or **hydropower**. Ancient Greeks and other preindustrial people used waterwheels to harness hydropower. A waterwheel collects water cascading downstream in buckets located around the wheel. The weight of the water causes the wheel to turn and changes the kinetic energy into mechanical energy, which is then used to grind wheat into flour or to pump water. Modern hydropower plants harness the kinetic energy of water as it cascades down a cliff face, as at Niagara Falls, or down a dam wall. Water released from a reservoir travels through the dam and spins the blades of a turbine. The turbine then turns a generator that produces electricity.

Hydroelectric power has many advantages over the two other main power sources, fossil-fuel and nuclear power. (**Fossil fuels** are ancient plants that have been transformed into oil, gas, or coal.) Streams will always flow; therefore, hydroelectric power is renewable. **Renewable resources** can be harvested without being completely used up. (By contrast, **nonrenewable resources** are not replenished on a human timescale.) Hydroelectric power is pollutant free. Fossil fuels release air pollutants, and nuclear power generates excess heat and potentially dangerous waste products.

Hydropower plants produce about 24% of the world's electricity. Almost all of the world's major rivers are dammed, most in several places in their courses. Since 1950, the number of large dams over 50 feet (15 m) in height has increased from 5,700 worldwide to more than 41,000. Still, many developing nations have great untapped hydropower potential.

In industrialized nations, hydroelectric power is especially important in mountainous regions with heavy rainfall. Nearly all the rivers in the United States have been dammed. (The longest remaining undammed river is the nearly 700 mile- (1,200 km-) long Yellowstone River in Montana.) About 2,000 hydropower plants generate 13% of the electricity in the contiguous United States, an amount that is estimated to be about 75% of the potential hydropower. This is down from 33% in the 1940s. Some countries, such as Norway and Sweden, get nearly 100% of their electricity from hydropower.

Besides harnessing power, dams lessen or prevent flooding. If a reservoir behind a dam is less than full, it can hold excess water and protect the area downstream from flooding. To shield all the areas along a floodplain, engineers use other obstructions, such as levees, which are concrete barriers built on the side of a river bank to wall in a rising stream. While levees protect the land behind them, floodwaters may rush past the levees and strike the unprotected bank downstream with even greater force. Levees constrict a rising river instead of allowing it to spread over its floodplain. This constriction actually forms a partial dam that causes waters upstream to rise. During especially large floods, levees may be topped by floodwater. Because they are often not built to withstand the most damaging floods, levees sometimes break or collapse. With luck, the excess water from a collapsing levee can be channeled down a spillway.

Levees keep a stream from depositing sediment on the floodplain, so, instead, the sediment remains in the channel. However, over time, the base of the channel may rise above the surrounding land, bringing about the potential of a disastrous flood if the levee is breached. The Mississippi River, for example, lies above New Orleans and is held back by levees. So while levees may solve the problem of flooding in the short term, they may create more destructive floods in the long term. Also, when the river drops its sediment in its channel instead of carrying it out to the wetlands, the wetlands become sediment starved and erode. Loss of sediment has been the main reason for wetlands loss in Louisiana.

The construction of levees and dams may increase the risk of flooding. When people are convinced that a levee system will protect their property from flooding, development may blossom. However, this development becomes vulnerable to large floods, such as those that occurred along the Mississippi River in 1993 and in New Orleans after Hurricane Katrina in 2005.

The Disadvantages of Dams

There are many advantages to dams: They provide reliable sources of water, protect areas from floods, and supply clean power. But dams and reservoirs also cause problems. In semiarid and arid regions, water easily evaporates from reservoirs and the canals that come from them. This results in the loss of water and the concentration of salts. If this brackish water is used for irrigation, the salts collect in the soil, which causes **salinization** (the addition of salt to the soil) of the farm-land. Reservoir water is lost in all climates due to seepage into the bedrock and leakage from irrigation ditches. Rivers deposit sediment in the reservoir, causing the lake to fill up over time.

Stopping floods can also interrupt important processes. Before the Aswan Dam in Egypt was built, for example, the Nile River flooded each spring, bringing in new, nutrient-rich soil for farmers to culti-vate. Without annual replenishment, the soil has become depleted in nutrients and must be fertilized, something that is too expensive for many of the subsistence farmers of the Nile Valley.

Dams block fish from migrating upstream. Dams on the Columbia River and its tributaries have contributed to the decimation of native salmon populations in the Pacific Northwest. Besides blocking the fishes' routes, dams change the temperature of the water downstream, usually to the detriment of the native species and the advantage of the nonnatives. Of 47 commercial species of fish in the Nile River, about 30 have become extinct or virtually so. Fisheries in the Nile Delta that once supported over a million people have been wiped out.

Diversion dams, along with periodic droughts in Africa's Sahel region, have shrunk Lake Chad from about 10,000 square miles

The 1993 Mississippi River Flood

The most devastating river flood in U.S. history was the 1993 Mississippi River flood. Rainfall that year over the Mississippi River basin was between two and six times the normal amount. Local streams overflowed as the ground became too saturated to absorb more rainwater. Since 80% of the basin's wetlands had been lost, floodwater storage capacity was drastically decreased. During the previous 70 years, 6,800 miles (11,000 km) of levees had been built along the banks of the Mississippi and its tributaries. But the flood was so big it caused 150 levees comprising over 6,000 miles (9,300 km) to fail. Nonetheless, levees did save low-lying areas in towns such as Davenport, Iowa; Rock Island, Illinois; and Hannibal, Missouri.

As a result of the flood:

- 48 people died
- 26,000 people were evacuated
- Over 56,000 homes were damaged
- Direct economic losses were $12 billion
- 250,000 people in Des Moines were without drinking water during the hot summer when the water treatment plant flooded
- 16,000 square miles (40,000 sq. km) of farmland were submerged and corn and soybean production decreased 5 to 9%
- Barge traffic halted for two months, seriously restricting the distribution of coal, petroleum, and grain
- Hundreds of miles of roads were closed.

As a result of the 1993 Mississippi flood, the U.S. Soil Conservation Service spent $25 million to buy floodplain farmlands to convert back into wetlands.

(25,000 sq. km) to just 770 square miles (2,000 sq. km) in the last three decades. The lake's once abundant fisheries have entirely collapsed.

Dams can also overflow or break, resulting in enormous property damage and fatalities. One infamous example is the 1928 St. Francis Dam disaster, near Los Angeles, California. One side of the 200-foot-high concrete dam was built into an old landslide, and the dam was constructed 20 feet (6.1 m) higher than its original design had specified. The day before the break, a leak was found in the dam, but it was ignored. When the structure crumpled, billions of gallons of water—a 78-foot-high wall of water at its peak—rushed down San Francisquito Canyon into the Santa Clara River Valley until it reached the Pacific Ocean, 54 miles (87 km) away. More than 450 people died (most were asleep, and many bodies were never found); 1,200 houses were destroyed; 10 bridges were knocked out; untold numbers of livestock were lost; and many communities lost power. The dam failure has been called the greatest American civil engineering failure of the twentieth century.

Hydroelectric dams must be built in suitable sites such as steep-walled canyons, which may be hard to find. Hydropower has decreased as a source of energy in the United States because all of the best sites have been used. Also, because dams and their reservoirs alter the canyon and the land behind it, possible dam sites are often rejected to protect the natural river and its canyon. This rejection became possible when electricity generated by fossil fuels became cheaper.

Dams alter the flow, temperature, and clarity of a stream, changing it from a flowing body of water to a stagnant one. A natural river tends to be fairly homogeneous in temperature. Water in a reservoir, however, is warmer on the top and colder on the bottom. Because water is usually released from the base of a dam, the river that flows below a dam is colder than the natural river. Temperature alterations may affect river life because the life cycles of many invertebrates are temperature dependent. A stonefly, for example, may need a certain temperature to begin metamorphosis. Even though the loss of flies may not seem important, the destruction of organisms low in a food web will affect all the animals that depend on those organisms directly or indirectly for survival. Thus, changes in conditions due to dams change a river's ecology.

Fish such as salmon, many trout, bass, shad, and some minnows migrate up rivers to reproduce. Dams make it difficult for the adults to swim up the river and for the offspring to swim down. This impedes reproduction, and eventually the fish on the river die out. Fish ladders, designed to assist fish in their migration up or down a dam, are not always successful. Juvenile fish often die by being caught in the dam's turbines or by falling from the reservoir to the river below. Dams release water in surges: large amounts when a lot of power is needed, such as during a warm summer day, and small amounts when less power is sufficient. These cyclic floods flush away the spawning gravel of salmon and steelhead trout during the day and leave it dry during the night, further reducing spawning success. (**Spawn** is the mass of eggs dropped by some female fish and invertebrates.)

The Colorado River once ran warm and muddy through the desert Southwest. Many dams have since been built on the river including the 1963 Glen Canyon Dam, which is located upstream from the entrance to the Grand Canyon, in northeastern Arizona. When the river emerges below the dam, it is sediment free, debris free, nearly nutrient free, and much colder. The area's ecosystem has suffered as native fish such as the Colorado squawfish (*Pytchocheilus lucius*), humpback chub (*Gila cypha*), and bonytail chub (*Gila elegans*) have been replaced by introduced trout and other game fish such as striped bass (*Morone saxatilis*), largemouth bass (*Micropterus salmoides*), and smallmouth bass (*Micropterus dolomieu)* in the reservoir and the river below the dam. Populations of several bird species, including the Southwestern Willow Flycatcher (*Empidomax traillii extimus*), have declined in the area in recent years.

Perennial rivers in arid regions, including the Colorado, are overused and now run dry during part of the year. This, too, brings many ecological changes, including loss of native species. So much water is diverted for human uses that the Colorado's water no longer reaches the sea year round. This also has happened with the Rio Grande, the Yellow River, the Amu Darya River, and other rivers.

The most infamous dam that was *never* built in the United States would have flooded the Grand Canyon within Grand Canyon National Park, Arizona. Although the dam would have been built between the large Glen Canyon Dam and the Hoover Dam, engineers and politicians insisted that it was needed. The government even suggested that the dam would not harm the natural beauty of the area but would raise water levels and allow tourists to float closer to the cliffs. The project was killed largely by a 1966 ad placed by the Sierra Club on a full page in *The New York Times* under the banner, "Should we also flood the Sistine Chapel, so tourists can get nearer the ceiling?"

Perhaps the most infamous dam in existence is the Three Gorges Dam on China's Yangtze River. This behemoth, scheduled for completion in 2009, will be the world's largest dam. At more than 600 feet

The Hetch Hetchy Controversy

The Yosemite Valley, in California's Yosemite National Park, is one of the most magnificent natural features in the world. Cascading waterfalls plummet down steep granite cliffs onto a nearly flat valley floor. Because of its spectacular scenery, Yosemite Valley is crowded on most days with some of the 4 million people who visit the park each year.

Submerged beneath 300 feet (90 m) of Tuolumne River water lies another valley, the Hetch Hetchy, which was dammed in 1923. Although a national park belongs to all the people of the United States, in 1913 Congress gave ownership of Hetch Hetchy Valley to San Francisco, California, to build a dam to supply its water and power. But not everyone was in favor of submerging this wilderness. The famous naturalist and environmentalist John Muir led the fight to save Hetch Hetchy. "It is a flood of singing air, water, and sunlight woven into cloth that spirits might wear," he wrote in *The Century Magazine* in 1890. Although Muir lost the battle for Hetch Hetchy, it was the first time significant numbers of people had risen up against "progress." The modern environmental movement was born.

Over the years, San Francisco has grown to depend on the Hetch Hetchy reservoir. The city draws 85% of its water and one-sixth of its electricity from Hetch Hetchy. A large portion of the water for counties surrounding the city also comes from Hetch Hetchy. The water is so pure that the city does not filter it, and it travels much of the way to San Francisco by gravity. The city sells some of the hydropower it generates to other users for around $50 million a year.

Although the idea of removing the dam has long been at the fringes of the environmental movement, the idea has caught on with more mainstream politicians. In 1987, Secretary of the Interior Donald Hodel (under President Ronald Reagan) suggested that the dam be removed and the valley restored. Republican California Assemblyman Tim Leslie told the *Sacramento Bee* in 2004, "Restoring [Hetch Hetchy] would be a priceless gift to future generations, not only for Californians but for all Americans."

But the issue is complicated. San Francisco could likely replace Hetch Hetchy water with water from two small reservoirs it owns on the Tuolumne River, with water from the very large New Don

(183 m) high and 1.5 miles (2.4 km) wide, the dam will create a reservoir hundreds of feet deep and nearly 400 miles (650 km) long. The turbines will create as much electricity as 18 nuclear power plants

Hetch Hetchy valley and its reservoir, showing the "bathtub ring" that marks the high water level. The valley's granite cliffs greatly resemble nearby Yosemite Valley. (© Galen Rowell, http://www.mountainlight.com)

Pedro reservoir downstream, or by building a larger reservoir nearer to the city (although this water would not have Hetch Hetchy's purity). Replacing the hydropower with power from coal- or petroleum-fired plants would increase the emission of pollutants and climate-altering **greenhouse gases**. These changes would be costly: an estimated $3 billion to $10 billion, according to a 2006 State of California study.

Although there is no easy resolution to this controversy, the federal government has proposed to undertake a study into options for Hetch Hetchy beginning in 2008.

or 15 coal-burning plants. Part of the reason for the project is to end the Yangtze's massive floods, which have killed more than one million people in the past century.

The dam's cost, though, is great. The rising waters will flood 395 square miles (632 sq. km) of land, displacing 1.2 million people from nearly 500 cities, towns, and villages along the river. Magnificent scenery and irreplaceable architectural and archeological sites will be lost, including ancestral burial sites, temples dating back hundreds of years, and even fossil locales. More than 300,000 farmers will need to be relocated, but because the Yangtze's floodplains are among the most fertile land in China, the replacement land is unlikely to be as productive. Alterations of river conditions will further endanger baiji dolphins (*Lipotes vexillifer*) and finless porpoises (*Neophocaena phocaenoides*), among other creatures. The price tag for the dam may rise as high as $50 billion.

Dam Removal

Dams have a limited lifespan, and each year in the United States tens of hundreds of small dams are removed when they become too expensive to maintain. Even a useful dam may be eliminated when its environmental costs are determined to be too high. Two dams on the Elwha River in Olympic National Park in Washington State are scheduled to be torn down in 2008 to restore the salmon fishery, which was reduced to a trickle when the dams were built in the early 1900s. The river was once one of the most productive salmon fisheries in the Pacific Northwest, a spawning ground for all five species of Pacific salmon and other fish. If successfully restored, the fishery will be worth an estimated $3 billion to $6 billion today.

WRAP-UP

The use of surface waters for drinking, irrigation, transportation, and other human needs has allowed civilization to develop. Cities that were established before the carving of extensive roadways had to be built along waterways or at ports that offered a connection between a landmass and the sea. Yet the engineering of waterways has often come at a price. Perhaps the important message from Hetch Hetchy is that decisions that affect the environment must be made with consideration of the long-term effects. This is also true of flood-control projects, in which protecting one location may place another in danger, or protecting a potentially hazardous location may encourage increased development, placing even more people and infrastructure at risk.

Groundwater and Its Use

Groundwater accounts for 22% of the world's freshwater, 36 times more than is present in all streams and lakes. In the United States, 20% of the water people use is groundwater, and as much as 85% of that water is used to grow food. Despite its abundance, groundwater is being overused in many areas, as will be seen in this chapter.

WHAT IS GROUNDWATER?

Water is almost everywhere under the ground, but it is only usable if it is contained in an **aquifer**. Not all rocks and sediments make good aquifers. First, the material must have holes or cracks, a feature known as **porosity**. Soil usually has high porosity, about 55%. Rocks are generally less porous than soil, although their porosity differs greatly. For example, hard rocks, such as granite, have between 5% and 40% porosity, depending on the extent to which they are fractured. Other porous rocks include partially dissolved limestone (10%

to 30% porosity) and sandstone (5 to 30%). Besides high porosity, an aquifer must have good **permeability**, which refers to the interconnectedness of the pores and cracks. Fractured rocks often have good

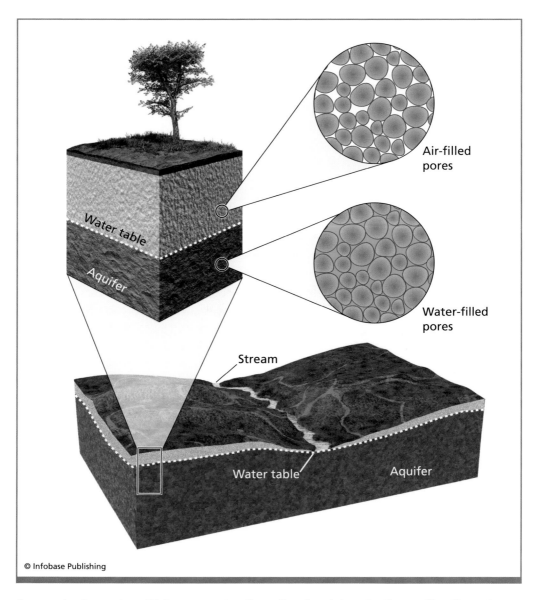

Air-filled pores

Water-filled pores

Stream

Water table

Aquifer

Water table

Aquifer

© Infobase Publishing

A groundwater system. Water permeates the soil and rock to enter the aquifer; the water table is the line separating the rock with air-filled pores and the rock with water-filled pores.

permeability, but clay, although it is porous, has low permeability because the holes are not interconnected.

Aquifers are recharged by water that seeps into the ground, often from a lake or a wetland area. Like surface water, groundwater usually flows downhill, traveling with the slope of the water table. Groundwater flows toward, and eventually into, streams, rivers, lakes, wetlands, and the oceans.

The **water table** is the level in an aquifer above which its pores are filled with air and below which they are filled with water. During the wet season, rain seeps into the ground to refill the aquifer, and the water table rises. During the dry season, the water table falls. In humid regions, the water table intersects the ground surface to feed streams or lakes. Aquifers supply water to streams even when there has been no rain. In arid regions, the water table is well below the ground surface, so desert streambeds are usually dry.

Groundwater flows through the aquifer at different rates depending on the permeability and porosity of the rock or soil. Groundwater may move as an underground river through dissolved limestone. However, groundwater ordinarily moves through an aquifer slowly, only about 1.5 inches (4 cm) per day, 5 feet (15 m) per year. The amount of time a water molecule spends in a groundwater aquifer varies, based on the aquifer's porosity, its slope, and the distance the water travels. The amount of time varies from days or weeks to 10,000 or more years. By contrast, a water molecule spends about two weeks in a river.

Water percolating through soil and rock is filtered, so groundwater is naturally quite pure. Filtering, combined with the large amounts of time the water spends underground, frees most groundwater of **pathogens** (disease-causing microscopic viruses, bacteria, and simple, single-celled organisms called protozoans), sediments, and some pollutants. The exact makeup of the water depends on the chemistry of the water and of the rock that hosts the aquifer.

Groundwater gushes and seeps onto the land's surface at springs. At hot springs, the dynamics of water flow can cause a spectacular display. In Yellowstone National Park the water in some of the hot springs is trapped until the pressure builds high enough to blow the steaming water through a constriction in the rock and erupt as a geyser. Old Faithful, Yellowstone's most famous geyser, erupts approximately every 80 minutes.

GROUNDWATER ECOSYSTEMS

The resources necessary for life are virtually absent in a groundwater system. There is water, but there is no light, little oxygen, and scant nutrients. However, life was recently discovered in some aquifers, inhabiting the dark spaces between sand grains. Called **stygobionts** (in reference to the River Styx, one of the five rivers in the Ancient Greek mythological underworld), the creatures are mostly invertebrates. Stygobionts are found in porous groundwater aquifers and in karst features, which are landforms created by limestone that has been dissolved in groundwater.

As organisms that have adapted to their extreme environment, stygobionts are colorless, eyeless, and have worm-shaped bodies for easier movement. As compared with typical aquatic organisms, stygobionts move and metabolize more slowly and have longer life spans. Without light, there is no photosynthesis; therefore, their food energy comes into the ecosystem as organic matter from the surface. Because food is scarce, most stygobionts will eat whatever they can find—a good adaptation to have in an extreme environment.

GROUNDWATER USE

Groundwater is not as easy to use as surface water, but where there is an aquifer, it is always available, even in dry seasons. The springs that come from groundwater acquifers have long provided water to animals and humans in areas where there is no permanent surface water. Even in the Sahara Desert, springs support about 90 different oases—islands of life in a dry, harsh environment.

Groundwater is an abundant, year-round water source, provided the aquifer is accessible. All over the world, people drill wells directly into aquifers and pump water to cities, towns, and farms. The cost of

Fountain at the Bellagio Hotel in otherworldly Las Vegas, Nevada. The average annual rainfall of Las Vegas is 4 inches (10.2 cm). *(Dennis Flaherty / Photo Researchers, Inc.)*

the water depends on the depth of the water table and the type of rock the well must be drilled through. Due to the abundance of groundwater, even desert cities such as Las Vegas, Nevada, are able to use water in what many consider wasteful ways.

Groundwater exploitation causes problems. Because the water replenishes slowly, overuse of an aquifer causes the water table to fall and wells to run dry. The solution to the problem is to drill deeper, an expensive and sometimes difficult task. Ultimately, overuse may cause an aquifer to go dry or to become uneconomical to use.

Groundwater removal also causes **subsidence**, or sinking of the land surface. After water is removed from an aquifer, the weight of the overlying rock may collapse the voids left behind, causing the ground surface to sink. Where groundwater use is extreme, the land above the aquifer may collapse at a rate of 2 to 4 inches (5 to 10 cm) per year. Subsidence is partially responsible for the tilt of the Leaning Tower of Pisa, which currently leans at about 7 feet (2.25 m) off center: Its tilt is increasing 0.05 inches (1.2 mm) per year. Mexico City is built on old lakebeds and draws 80% of its water from the aquifers beneath it. As a result, the city, which is one of the largest and most populous in the world, has sunk an estimated 30 feet (9 m) in some locations.

In many locations in the world, including the United States, groundwater is being taken from aquifers much more rapidly than it is being recharged. Farmers depend on this water for their crops, and cities depend on it for their municipal water supplies. In the long term, the practice of groundwater mining is not sustainable. (Resource use that is **sustainable** does not compromise the current needs for resources or the resources that will be needed by future generations for present economic gain.)

Where there are hot springs, groundwater can be used as a source of energy. **Geothermal energy** is used for heating homes and generating electricity. Hot water and steam are pumped directly into houses via pipes or are used to turn turbine generators to produce electricity. Geothermal energy is renewable, and because no fuel is burned, no pollutants are released. In Iceland, about 87% of all houses are heated with geothermal energy, and only a small fraction of the energy available has been harnessed. The Geysers, a complex of geothermal power plants in northern California, is the largest producer of geothermal energy in the United States.

WRAP-UP

Groundwater is the most important source of freshwater because there is so much of it. Water from underground aquifers is often abundant, easy to obtain if the water table is not too deep, and relatively pure. Groundwater is available in arid locations where surface water is scarce. For these reasons, the groundwater supply is often overused. The Ogallala Aquifer in the midwestern United States is just one example of an aquifer that is being depleted far more rapidly

The Ogallala Aquifer

The midwestern United States is the breadbasket of America. For more than six decades, farming in the region has depended on irrigation water from the Ogallala Aquifer. The aquifer is a 15- to 30-foot-thick (50 to 100 m) layer of permeable sand and gravel that lies between 4.5 and 30 feet (15 and 100 m) below the surface. The aquifer stretches for 800 miles (1,300 km) through South Dakota, Wyoming, Nebraska, Colorado, Kansas, Oklahoma, Texas, and New Mexico.

The Ogallala Aquifer provides an estimated one-third of all irrigation water in the United States. The water is used to irrigate more than 14 million acres (57,000 sq. km) of land—an area about the size of Massachusetts, Vermont, and Connecticut combined. The major products are corn, wheat, cotton, and cattle. In addition, water from the aquifer is used for the region's cities and industries. On average, water is being pumped at eight times the rate that it is being recharged, and the water table is dropping, in some areas as much as 3 to 5 feet (90 to 150 cm) per year. Some hydrologists estimate that one-fourth of the aquifer's

The Ogallala Aquifer stretches for 800 miles (1,300 km) through South Dakota, Wyoming, Nebraska, Colorado, Kansas, Oklahoma, Texas, and New Mexico.

original supply of water will be depleted by 2020, and it may be completely spent in areas where the aquifer is shallow. Estimates for the aquifer's remaining lifespan vary from 60 to 220 years in different areas. If the aquifer is eventually exhausted, water will need to be brought in from elsewhere, at enormous cost, or the productivity of this farmland will diminish greatly.

than it is being replenished. If groundwater mining continues at its current rate, the aquifer will be unable to provide water for America's farmlands within several decades. Years of groundwater mining have resulted in subsidence of the land surface in many areas, particularly arid ones. In some areas, geothermal energy from groundwater is used as a source of electric power.

PART TWO

FRESHWATER POLLUTANTS AND THEIR EFFECTS

Where Water Pollutants Come From and Where They Go

This chapter describes the ways that surface water and groundwater can become polluted. Pollutants enter surface waters in fallout from the atmosphere, in **runoff** from the land, by water trickling through waste sites, or directly, from pipes, ships, and other sources. Groundwater becomes contaminated when polluted surface water trickles into an aquifer or when liquid infiltrates from leaking tanks or industrial waste sites. Once in the water, pollutants can be diluted, dispersed, or broken down. However, they may build up in the food web.

HOW SURFACE WATER BECOMES POLLUTED

Surface water pollution is an enormous problem in the United States and elsewhere around the world. According to the Natural Resources Defense Council, about one-third of rivers and one-half of lakes are unfit for swimming, fishing, and other uses. For example, 83% of the water along approximately 980 miles (1,570 km) of the Ohio River is withdrawn for use within five miles (8 km) downstream of effluent discharge from a wastewater treatment plant.

Pollutants enter surface water from a distinct, identifiable source or from an extensive, poorly defined region. Pollutants that originate at a single location, such as a pipe, ditch, tank, or sewer, are examples of **point source pollution**. Point sources are easy to identify and therefore are relatively easy to block. Point source pollutants can enter the water directly. Boats with outboard motors, Jet Skis, and other recreational watercraft release up to 30% of their fuel straight into the water. Ships on large lakes may leak oil or dump waste, sometimes inadvertently. Routine ship operations such as discharging ballast water (water that is used to stabilize a ship) can bring in nonnative plants and animals and cause the decline of native species.

A pipe transporting polluted water feeds directly into a river. *(© age fotostock / SuperStock)*

Pollutants that come from a larger area, such as a fertilized field, livestock feedlot, parking lot, roadway, or even the atmosphere, are examples of **non-point source pollution**. Because non-point source pollution comes from many polluters, it is much more difficult to regulate than is point source pollution. Some non-point sources of pollution are described below.

The Atmosphere

The atmosphere is an important part of the water cycle and the location of the planet's weather. This layer of life-giving gases is also the sink for the gaseous waste products of modern human society. These wastes create **air pollution,** the contamination of the atmosphere by gases and particles in quantities that may be harmful to human health and the environment. Air pollutants have a variety of ill effects, from raising global temperature, to destroying natural atmospheric processes, to causing damage to the environment and human health.

The burning of fossil fuel releases into the air enormous quantities of pollutants such as nitrogen dioxide (NO_2), sulfur dioxide (SO_2), carbon monoxide (CO), and **hydrocarbons** (organic compounds composed of hydrogen and carbon). These pollutants float through the atmosphere or are washed away by rain. Of particular concern to humans are **heavy metals** such as mercury and lead, which are wastes emitted from the combustion of coal and other materials. (A heavy metal is a metal with high specific gravity—that is, high weight for a given volume.) Sulfur and nitrogen from coal combustion form the acids that fall as **acid rain** and create acid streams and lakes. Acid rain is considerably more acidic than normal rainwater, which has a pH of around 5.6. Nitrogen wastes in the atmosphere create nitrates, which act as nutrients in the water.

Sewage

Anything that is flushed down a toilet, runs through a sink, or enters a sewer drain in the street becomes **sewage,** the waste matter that passes through sewers. Sewage is 95% water. The remaining 5% is mostly human waste but also includes oil, toxic chemicals, fertilizers, pharmaceuticals (drugs), pesticides, pathogens, and trash. The organic material is **biodegradable,** which means it can be broken down by bacteria into stable, nontoxic inorganic compounds, such as carbon dioxide (CO_2), water (H_2O), and ammonia. Pathogens, synthetic (man-made) chemicals, and most trash are not biodegradable.

Sewage may run raw into lakes and streams, or it may be treated. In industrialized nations, sewage goes through a sewage treatment plant before it is released into the environment. How these plants work is described in Chapter 10. But even where there are sewage treatment plants, the sewage is not always thoroughly cleansed. The sewage systems of many large cities are now old and overextended.

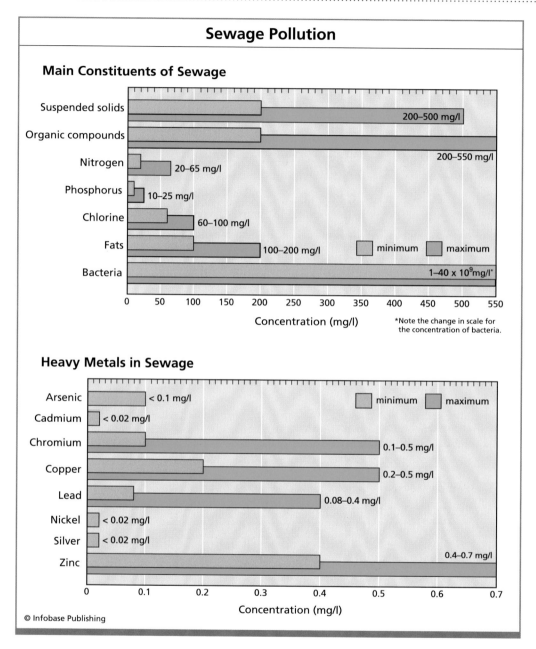

Sewage Pollution

Main Constituents of Sewage

Suspended solids — 200–500 mg/l
Organic compounds — 200–550 mg/l
Nitrogen — 20–65 mg/l
Phosphorus — 10–25 mg/l
Chlorine — 60–100 mg/l
Fats — 100–200 mg/l
Bacteria — $1\text{–}40 \times 10^9$ mg/l*

minimum   maximum

Concentration (mg/l)

*Note the change in scale for the concentration of bacteria.

Heavy Metals in Sewage

Arsenic — < 0.1 mg/l
Cadmium — < 0.02 mg/l
Chromium — 0.1–0.5 mg/l
Copper — 0.2–0.5 mg/l
Lead — 0.08–0.4 mg/l
Nickel — < 0.02 mg/l
Silver — < 0.02 mg/l
Zinc — 0.4–0.7 mg/l

minimum   maximum

Concentration (mg/l)

© Infobase Publishing

Sewage is defined as waste matter from domestic or industrial establishments that is carried away in sewers or drains. High concentrations of industrial and domestic waste entering natural water environments can disrupt ecosystems, while toxins and introduced pathogens may also affect human health.

Storms cause wastewater to overflow so that sewage is dumped directly into streams and lakes. Some pollutants, such as parasite eggs, nutrients, and synthetic organic chemicals, are not removed by the treatment regimen. Untreated sewage fouls the waters of many developed nations. In developing countries, sewage treatment costs are too high, and 90% of sewage enters inland waterways untreated. Large cities release hundreds of millions of tons of raw sewage into local waterways each year. Drinking or swimming in contaminated water results in hundreds of millions of cases of intestinal diseases each year. Diseases caused by polluted water will be discussed in Chapter 9.

Runoff

Water that flows across roadways and rooftops and over landfills and contaminated soil often drains directly into streams or lakes. This runoff can be contaminated with oil, with pollutants that were applied as pesticides or fertilizers, with chemicals from improperly maintained landfills, with pathogens from pet waste, with road salts, and with heavy metals from mines and other sources. According to the Environmental Protection Agency, polluted runoff is the greatest source of water quality problems in the United States.

"Sprawl [urban development] ruins water quality," James M. Tierney, the watershed inspector general for New York State, told *The New York Times* in 2007. "A good rule of thumb engineers use is that an acre of paved surface will have 15 times more runoff than an acre of natural forest or meadow." For each acre of a construction site, the runoff is 1,000 times that of a natural forest or meadow.

More cities are diverting roadway runoff to sewage treatment plants. However, the plants are unable to remove some kinds of pollutants, specifically fertilizers and other chemical compounds, which wind up running off into surface waters anyway.

Animal wastes enter surface water as runoff, primarily from animal feeding operations at factory farms. These farms are enormous production facilities: In some cases, hundreds of thousands of animals— pigs, cattle, dairy cows, and poultry—are crowded into a small area.

Polluted runoff from a shopping center parking lot in Inverness, Florida, is stored in a drainage pond. *(© Jeff Greenberg / The Image Works)*

The main purpose of factory farms is to grow animals for slaughter as quickly as possible. Farmers are contracted to grow the animals for large corporations, which take the product but leave behind the pollutants. These pollutants include nutrients in the waste and whatever chemicals or pharmaceuticals were used to facilitate raising the animals. Such pollutants may kill fish and other aquatic life and contaminate drinking-water supplies.

Although factory farms do not bear much resemblance to family farms, feeding operations work under laws that were designed for small farms that did not house enough animals to cause major environmental damage. Factory farms are major polluters because of the sheer numbers of animals they raise and process. In all, the feedlots in the United States produce nearly 300 billion pounds (136 million metric tons) of manure daily. North Carolina farms raise about 10 million hogs for slaughter, mostly in the east-central part of the state. On a typical farm, between 880 and 1,220 animals live together in a barn with slatted floors where the waste can pass through. When operations are working correctly, some of the organic material is biodegraded by bacteria in wastewater lagoons. These wastes, which are rich in phosphates and nitrates, are then sprayed on fields as fertilizer. Some operations produce more manure than they have lagoon space for, so they spread some of it on farmland. Unfortunately, the crops cannot absorb all those nutrients, so the excess runs off into the water supply.

Leaks are caused by faulty pond construction or inadequate maintenance. Spills usually occur when floodwaters cause the lagoons to

Chickens in a modern egg farm in Idaho. Animals packed so tightly together produce an incredible amount of waste. (© David Frazier / The Image Works)

overflow. If the waste generated exceeds the facility's capacity, it is not uncommon for farms to discharge the waste illegally. Recommendations on how to decrease the amount of pollution coming from factory farms are given in Chapter 11.

Industrial Waste

Industrial waste may be piped into surface water directly, or it may be stored in ponds and contaminated waste sites. Water trickling through disposal areas brings contaminants to streams, lakes, ponds, and groundwater. Many waste disposal sites were built before regulations were in place. Others are improperly maintained, and there is often little enforcement. An example of an industrial waste disaster, the Love Canal waste site, is discussed in Chapter 10.

HOW GROUNDWATER BECOMES POLLUTED

Groundwater is less likely to be polluted than surface water. Pollutants are filtered out of the water as they seep down through the soil and rock above the aquifer or travel slowly through the aquifer. But the ability of soil and rock to remove pollutants from groundwater varies widely depending on the pollutants and the rock type. As a result, up to 25% of the total usable groundwater and about 45% of the municipal groundwater supply in the United States is contaminated.

Pollutants in groundwater come primarily from the same sources as those in surface waters. Water standing in ponds and lakes or in agricultural fields filters through the soil and rock into the aquifer. Groundwater is especially susceptible to toxins stored in landfills and underground storage tanks. More than 100,000 underground storage tanks in the United States are leaking, and millions more will develop leaks. Once pollutants are in an aquifer, they spread as a plume of contamination away from the source. The plume moves as slowly as the water in the aquifer, as little as a few inches a day.

Wells in 38 states contain pesticide levels high enough to threaten human health. In New Jersey, every major aquifer is contaminated. In

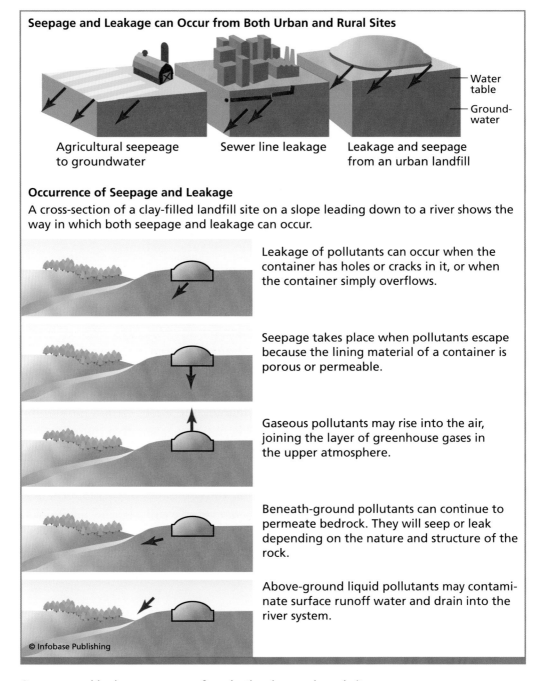

Seepage and Leakage can Occur from Both Urban and Rural Sites

Agricultural seepeage to groundwater

Sewer line leakage

Leakage and seepage from an urban landfill

Water table

Ground-water

Occurrence of Seepage and Leakage

A cross-section of a clay-filled landfill site on a slope leading down to a river shows the way in which both seepage and leakage can occur.

Leakage of pollutants can occur when the container has holes or cracks in it, or when the container simply overflows.

Seepage takes place when pollutants escape because the lining material of a container is porous or permeable.

Gaseous pollutants may rise into the air, joining the layer of greenhouse gases in the upper atmosphere.

Beneath-ground pollutants can continue to permeate bedrock. They will seep or leak depending on the nature and structure of the rock.

Above-ground liquid pollutants may contaminate surface runoff water and drain into the river system.

© Infobase Publishing

Seepage and leakage can occur from both urban and rural sites.

Florida, where 92% of the people drink groundwater, over 90% of the wells have detectable levels of industrial and agricultural chemicals, and more than 1,000 wells have been closed.

WHAT HAPPENS TO POLLUTANTS IN THE WATER

Water pollutants may find their way out of the water or may be diluted, dispersed, or broken down. Pollutants in surface waters can leave a water body by flowing from one reservoir to another, as from a stream into a lake or the ocean. Some adhere to sediments that fall through the water and settle on the lake bottom. Eventually, these sediments, along with the pollutants, are buried by other sediments.

A polluted body of water will be diluted by rainwater or water from other streams, and these two types of water will be mixed by currents and waves. Bacteria will biodegrade organic pollutants, which make up the largest volume of waste, over time. This organic material acts as fertilizer in an ecosystem; if a lot of waste is added, the bacteria population explodes. **Aerobic** bacteria, which need oxygen, consume the waste until the oxygen runs out. **Anaerobic** bacteria, which do not need oxygen, then degrade the waste further, producing the byproducts hydrogen sulfide (the rotten-egg smell of rotting waste) and methane.

Nonbiodegradable compounds may break apart or become ionized, may dissolve, or may combine with other chemicals to form new compounds. Some of these new compounds will also be hazardous. For example, a pesticide may break down into compounds that are more widely harmful to the environment than the original chemical. The insecticide dichlorodiphenyltrichloroethane (DDT) serves as an example of this process.

Some pollutants remain unchanged in the water. When water evaporates, chemicals that are left behind, like salts, become concentrated. Compounds may undergo **bioaccumulation** in the aquatic food web. First, zooplankton take in a small amount of a substance from the water. Then, small fish accumulate all of the substance from all of the zooplankton they eat. Next, larger fish accumulate all of the substance from all of the small fish they eat, and so on. Animals in the upper levels of the food web, the top predators, may accumulate enormous concentrations of the compounds and store them in their body fat. If the animals metabolize the fat (for example, during lean times), the toxic compounds enter the animals' systems. Substances that have

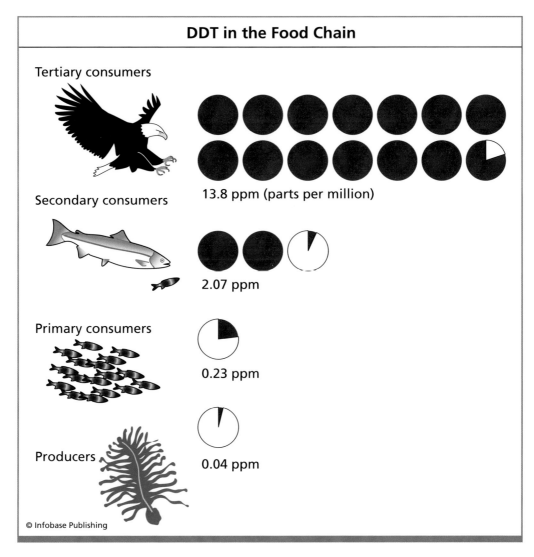

DDT in the Food Chain

Tertiary consumers

13.8 ppm (parts per million)

Secondary consumers

2.07 ppm

Primary consumers

0.23 ppm

Producers

0.04 ppm

© Infobase Publishing

The diagram shows how DDT becomes concentrated in the tissues of organisms representing four successive trophic levels in a food chain.

little noticeable effect in small animals may cause great damage in large predators because the substances become so concentrated. By contrast, aspirin does not bioaccumulate. A person can take the recommended dose of aspirin each day and have only that small dose within his or her body. But a small daily dose of mercury bioaccumulates so that in time a person's body contains a large amount of mercury, eventually resulting in neurological problems and even death.

WRAP-UP

Water pollutants enter freshwater systems directly from the source or from the atmosphere, sewage, or runoff. Once in the water, the pollutants may be diluted, dispersed, or broken down. Alternatively, they may remain or even build up in the environment so that they cause damage to people or to the ecosystem in which they are found. Chapter 6 will discuss the health effects pollutants have on humans and on wildlife.

Possible Health Effects
of Toxic Chemicals

This chapter discusses the possible health effects of toxic chemicals. (The chemicals themselves are discussed in Chapters 7 and 8.) The separation of the two topics is necessary because most health effects are brought about by more than one type of chemical. Toxic chemicals are synthetic compounds that are certainly, or likely, harmful to humans or wildlife. These compounds can lead to physiological disorders such as reproductive problems that include infertility or spontaneous abortion (miscarriage), developmental abnormalities, neurological disorders, immune system problems, and many other disorders. Some are **carcinogens**, chemical substances or physical entities (e.g., X-rays or ultraviolet radiation) that cause cells to grow uncontrollably—that is, they cause **cancer**. Even now, the effects of many compounds are not known, nor is it known what effects on health the combination of two or more compounds might have.

UNDERSTANDING THE HEALTH EFFECTS OF WATER POLLUTION

Understanding the health effects of various pollutants in humans is extremely difficult. The obvious way to go about learning about these effects would be to deliberately expose large numbers of people to a toxin and then analyze the response. For good reasons, this approach is unethical and is not practiced.

Two less direct, but more ethical, approaches have been developed for analyzing the health effects of pollutants on people: epidemiological studies and animal studies. **Epidemiology** is the field of medicine concerned with the study of **epidemics**, which are outbreaks of disease that affect large numbers of people. While medical doctors study symptoms in a single patient, epidemiologists study disease outbreaks in populations. When a cluster of people with a particular disease is discovered, the patients are surveyed to identify possible causes. For example, if a higher than normal incidence of brain cancer is discovered among the children of a town, epidemiologists will survey the families for possible causes. As a result of the survey, the researchers may discover, for example, that all the sick children drink water from the same well.

There are several problems with using epidemiological approaches to determine the effects of toxins on human health:

- The disease is already in the population. In the instance of brain cancer, although future cases may be prevented, the children who have the disease are already sick.
- Many diseases, especially cancer, may not appear until one or more decades after the exposure, allowing the contamination to spread to many people.
- If more than one pollutant may be causing the disease, researchers find it difficult to determine which one is the culprit or if there is more than one cause. Uncovering the toxic dose is also difficult.

Despite these limitations, epidemiological studies are extremely useful for identifying the causes of diseases and for instigating cleanup efforts.

A Civil Action

The 1995 book *A Civil Action* (which was made into a 1998 film starring John Travolta) chronicles an epidemiological study unintentionally carried out by a mother. When Anne Anderson's son Jimmy developed childhood leukemia (cancer of the white blood cells) when he was three, she wondered about the other children she knew who also had the disease. She ultimately identified a cluster of 12 cases in and around her neighborhood of Woburn, Massachusetts. The childhood leukemia rate in the city overall was four times than expected for a city of its size. Rates of other cancers were high as well. Anderson wondered whether her well water, which was foul smelling and discolored the pipe fittings, could be responsible. She learned that hundreds of acres of marshy land in North Woburn were heavily contaminated with lead, arsenic, and chromium. Eventually, two of the city's wells were found to be contaminated and were closed. *A Civil Action* is an exciting tale of the attempt to connect the pollution with the cancers and to take legal action against the polluters. Anderson's son ultimately died from his disease.

In addition to epidemiological studies, laboratory experiments are performed to estimate the effects of a pollutant on humans. In some experiments, a suspected toxin is introduced to cells in a dish. More commonly, lab animals, usually rats, are exposed to high levels of a suspected toxin, and their response is recorded. For several reasons, these studies yield imperfect results. The rats' response to the toxins may not be the same as it would be in humans. Also, because researchers want their results on a useful time scale, the animals are usually fed large doses of the toxin over a short period of time. This approach raises questions on the effectiveness of these types of studies: Will humans react to the toxin in the same way as the rats? Will the same dose, adjusted for body size, cause the same problem? If a large dose of the toxin over a short time brings on a disease in the rat (single exposure), will ingesting small amounts of the same toxin over a much longer period (chronic exposure) cause the same disease in humans? Although these questions are difficult to answer, animal studies are as close to studying the effect of toxins on humans as scientists can get.

WHO IS MOST AT RISK?

Not everyone is equally at risk for suffering from the diseases caused by water pollution. Illness and death rates from toxic pollutants depend on the health and age of the affected person. No matter what their age, people with such chronic health problems as compromised immune systems are more susceptible to the water-caused illnesses than are healthy adults. The elderly are at increased risk of illness because additional problems caused by pollution may exacerbate the health problems they already have.

Most deaths from water pollutants and pathogens occur in children under five years of age. Children are the most vulnerable to toxic chemicals because growing bodies take in substances more rapidly than do mature ones. Also, they take in a greater amount of food and liquid and are not able to detoxify and eliminate contaminants as efficiently as adults can. Three crucial stages in human development are before conception, during pregnancy, and during the early months after birth. Increasingly, evidence indicates that some childhood cancers result from damage that occurred in a parent's sperm or egg during exposure to chemicals such as solvents or pesticides. During gestation, hazardous chemicals cross the placenta, resulting in exposure of the growing fetus to compounds circulating through the mother's bloodstream. Nursing infants take in compounds contained in the mother's breast milk. While these toxin levels may not be high enough to cause problems in an adult, they can bring about illness or spontaneous abortion in the fetus or illness in the nursing infant.

CANCER

Cancer is not a single disease, but a group of more than 100 distinct diseases. The unifying trait of all cancers is the uncontrolled growth of abnormal cells in the body. Although some cancers are treated successfully, cancer is the cause of one in every four deaths in the United States. Nearly 40% of the people who receive a cancer diagnosis succumb to the disease within five years.

Chemical or physical factors can cause cancer. Chemical carcinogens include chemical emissions from industry, pollutants from cars and homes, and tobacco smoke. Physical carcinogens include ultraviolet radiation from sunlight and ionizing radiation from X rays and radioactive materials. A number of viruses can cause cancer, as can repeated local injury or recurring irritation to a part of the body. The ability of a carcinogen to cause cancer in an individual also depends on factors such as the person's general health and genetic makeup. Individuals with a genetic predisposition to cancer carry one or more genes that make them more vulnerable to the disease than individuals in the general population.

Adult cancers are ordinarily the result of years of collective damage to cells. The most common adult cancers—skin, prostate, breast, lung, and colon—are not found in children. Childhood cancers are thought to be the result of exposure to toxins during the periods of

Top Five Cancers in Adult Men and Adult Women

MALE, MOST COMMON	PERCENTAGE OF TOTAL	FEMALE, MOST COMMON	PERCENTAGE OF TOTAL
Prostate	29	Breast	26
Lung	15	Lung	15
Colorectal	10	Colorectal	11
Bladder	7	Uterine	6
Non-Hodgkin's lymphoma	4	Non-Hodgkin's lymphoma	4

Source: American Cancer Society

Childhood Cancers

CHILDHOOD CANCER	PERCENTAGE OF ALL CANCERS
Leukemia	32
Central nervous system, including brain	20
Lymphomas, including Hodgkin's disease and non-Hodgkin's lymphoma	11
Nerve, including neuroblastoma	8
Soft tissue sarcoma	7
Kidney	6
Bone	5

Source: American Cancer Society

growth described above. For this reason, 40% of childhood cancers occur in children under five, and most of those are in children less than one year old. Cancer rates decrease in later childhood but rise again in adolescence.

Childhood cancers are relatively rare. They account for only 2% of the total cancer cases in the United States. Still, cancer kills more children than anything else besides injuries. Childhood cancer rates have risen over the past few decades: about 1.8% per year for brain cancer and 1% per year for leukemia. Due to improved treatments, rising illness rates have corresponded with decreasing death rates for most childhood cancers. Brain cancer is the exception: Here, death rates have doubled in the last 25 years. The rates of the different cancers in children vary with age.

The difficulty of assigning blame for an illness to a particular cause is illustrated by epidemiological studies of childhood cancers. Different types of childhood cancer have been linked to different environmental factors, but the most danger appears to originate from pesticides, solvents, and radiation. Because pesticides and solvents are found in water, they will be discussed in this chapter.

Numerous research studies have linked pesticide exposure and childhood cancer. Still, many pesticides that have caused cancer in laboratory animals are still in use. Epidemiological studies have linked many forms of childhood cancer to pesticides used in the home and garden, applied at parents' workplaces, and sprayed on pets to control fleas. Children exposed to multiple products are especially vulnerable. Studies have demonstrated increases in childhood leukemia connected to pesticide use within a house and in the garden.

Solvents have been linked to brain tumors and leukemia, mostly due to exposure of the children's parents to the chemicals at their workplaces. Parents whose employment involves metalworking, painting, or motor-vehicle repair, or those who work in the personal-care product or chemical industries, pose the worst risk for children. Elevated leukemia rates were found in children whose parents were exposed to mixed solvents, chlorinated solvents, and three specific chemicals: benzene, carbon tetrachloride (largely banned today), and trichloroethylene (TCE).

Cancer is also known in animals: It can be induced in laboratory experiments, and it is found in nature. Cancer is normally rare in cetaceans—whales, dolphins, and porpoises—but beluga whales in the heavily polluted St. Lawrence estuary (part of the Great Lakes system) have a cancer rate similar to that of humans, domestic cats, and cattle: 27% of dead beluga whales in the estuary were found to have cancer, although not all died of the disease. Among this group of whales was the first case of breast cancer ever seen in a cetacean. Beluga whales eat small invertebrates they dig out of the sediments. The chemicals found in the sediments may make the whales especially vulnerable. Cancer rates among humans living near the estuary are higher than those in the rest of Quebec and Canada: Epidemiological studies have linked some incidences of cancer to toxic chemicals in the region.

Some scientists suspect that some cancers may be linked to tiny amounts of chemicals in the water supply. Current studies show that the incidence of some cancers may rise when a population is exposed to small amounts of certain chemicals, but the effect is slight. Another topic that is not well understood is how more than one pollutant or environmental stress may interact to cause cancer. In a study of men in Shanghai, China, those who consumed high doses of aflatoxin, a carcinogen produced by mold on peanuts, had four times the rate of liver cancer as other men. Men with hepatitis B infections of the liver had seven times the rate of liver cancer. Men with both risk factors—exposure to aflatoxin and diagnosis of hepatitis B—had 70 times the rate of liver cancer. These dramatic results show that carcinogens can amplify each other.

ENDOCRINE DISRUPTION

Researchers typically have concentrated on cancer when evaluating the health risks of pollutants. In recent years, other serious health effects have come to light, and they are receiving increasing amounts of study. The most important of these is the interruption of the **endocrine system**, known as endocrine disruption. The endocrine system regulates many of the body's functions, including growth, development, and maturation, by sending out hormones as chemical messengers. Hormones are released into the blood stream in carefully measured amounts by the endocrine glands, including the pituitary, thyroid, adrenal, thymus, pancreas, ovaries, and testes. Each type of hormone travels until it reaches a cell with a receptor into which it fits, like a key in a lock. This allows the hormone to "turn on" the cell, stimulating it to produce a certain protein or to multiply.

One example of a hormone is **estrogen**, the vertebrate female sex hormone that triggers the development of the sex organs and controls the reproductive cycle. Estrogen receptors are found in the uterus, breasts, brain, and liver, among other locations. Estrogen in the uterus causes the walls to thicken to allow for the possible implantation of a fertilized egg.

Hormones are especially important in the growth of young organisms. In mammals, birds, reptiles, and amphibians the development

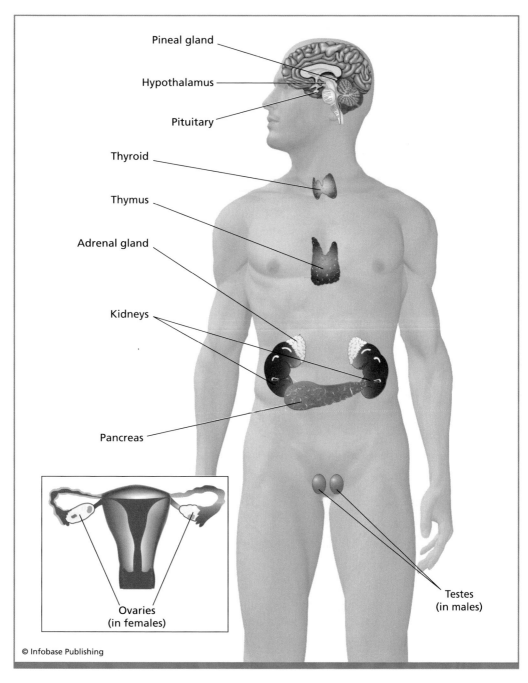

Each of the endocrine organs, illustrated above, produces one or more hormones. Some organs of the endocrine system, such as the pancreas and kidneys, have additional functions unrelated to hormone production.

of the fertilized egg into a healthy young organism depends on minute amounts of hormones carrying out their function at the right time. Too much or too little thyroid hormone at a certain time will permanently damage the brain of a developing mammal. Hormone disruption can also damage immune systems. Only miniscule amounts of a hormone are necessary for it to do its work, often as small as parts per billion (ppb) or parts per trillion (ppt). (*One part per billion* is one part out of one billion equally sized parts; *one part per trillion* is one part out of one trillion parts. In comparison, *percent* can be thought of as parts per hundred.)

The key-in-the-lock analogy for hormones and their receptors is not entirely accurate because the lock (the receptor) is fairly open and may accept more than one key. In the human body, there is ordinarily only one "key" hormone for each receptor type. But some receptors respond to chemicals manufactured outside the body. The estrogen receptor allows so many chemicals to bind to it that it has been called "promiscuous."

Chemicals manufactured outside the body that mimic hormones and interfere with the normal functions of the endocrine system are called **endocrine disruptors**. Because hormones are effective in such tiny quantities, endocrine disruptors need only be present in water in miniscule quantities to cause damage to living creatures. An endocrine disruptor might block a hormone from doing its job in a receptor. It might also give a signal that is too strong, causing the cell to do something it should not do, or to do what it should do but at the wrong time. It might even result in a signal that is too weak and also comes at the wrong time. Any part of the endocrine system can be tampered with by endocrine disruptors. Most of the endocrine disrupting chemicals in the environment are estrogens or compounds that mimic estrogens. Endocrine disruptors also interfere with **androgens**, which are male sex hormones, and with thyroid hormones.

The environment is awash in synthetic compounds that are potential endocrine disruptors. Sewage effluent contains high concentrations of man-made estrogens, primarily from birth control pills and estrogen replacement therapies (sometimes used during and after menopause), both of which are among the most prescribed pharmaceuticals in the United States. Pharmaceuticals enter the water system in many ways. Up to 90% of the dose of some medications may pass unaltered through a person's body.

"Just about everything people put into their mouth eventually gets into the water," Christian Daughton of the Environmental Protection Agency told *The New York Times* in 2005. People flush old prescriptions down the toilet. Drugs given to livestock, a common practice in factory farms, run off into the waterways. Water trickling through poorly engineered landfills picks up the medications disposed there and carries them into groundwater systems. These chemicals are not altered or stopped by sewage treatment facilities, do not adsorb onto sediments, and are not biodegradable. Endocrine disruptors are environmentally persistent—they remain in the environment for long time periods—and many bioaccumulate.

Aquatic animals get the brunt of damage from exposure to endocrine disruptors; an example is the misshapen and undersized sex organs they develop. Male fish exposed to environmental estrogens may develop smaller testes, have reduced sperm production, develop ovaries and produce eggs, or develop as females. **Feminization** is the process whereby a male takes on the traits of a female. After the parents' exposure to environmental estrogens, the numbers of males and females born may be skewed, with many more males than females or more females than males. The young may develop poorly, or the population may be reduced. In mammals, males exposed to estrogens do not develop correctly sexually or have limited reproductive success.

In a United States Geological Survey study performed in fall 2006, scientists working on three tributaries of the Potomac River found that more than 80% of male smallmouth bass (*Micropterus dolomieu*) were growing eggs inside their testes. The fish were swimming in water that contained three possible endocrine disruptors: a synthetic estrogen that is the active ingredient in birth control pills; triclosan, a disinfectant used in soap; and trifluralin, a pesticide used on farms. Water from the river runs through municipal water systems that remove most, but not all, of these chemicals.

In an October 2005 experiment, scientists at Baylor University placed caged fathead minnows (*Pimephales promelas*) downstream of a wastewater plant in Pecan Creek in Denton, Texas. Effluent from the plant contained low levels of synthetic estrogens. After three months in the stream, the males looked like females: their sexual organs had shrunk, the fat behind their heads was reduced, and the distinctive vertical gray lines on their sides had disappeared. Gender problems in fish are not limited by species or country. In the Netherlands, 37% of male freshwater bream (*Abramis brama*) had gonads with both male and female parts.

Male fish are not the only organisms that are altered by endocrine disruptors. Exposed male birds, mammals, and reptiles become feminized, and female fish, birds, mammals, and reptiles become more masculine, a process called **masculinization**. All of the organisms have reproductive system problems and decreased fertility. Studies have found cormorants suffering from cross-bill syndrome, in which their bills are crossed and useless; terns exhibiting birth defects from endocrine disruptors; fish with large tumors; and three-legged frogs.

It is known that humans also experience health effects from endocrine disruptors due to the tragic case of the synthetic estrogen DES (diethylstilbestrol). In the years between 1938 and 1971, DES was given to pregnant women who were experiencing pregnancy complications. The goal was to boost estrogen to prevent miscarriage (it was later found that DES actually induces miscarriage). Adult women whose mothers took DES have suffered rare cancers, deformed reproductive organs, and increased risk of endometriosis, a condition in which small pieces of the lining of the uterus migrate to other places in the pelvic area. Adult male children have experienced some reproductive disorders, as well. While the concentrations of synthetic hormones circulating in the environment today are much lower than the doses of DES given to the pregnant women, evidence suggests that problems similar to DES damage still may be occurring.

Exposure to some pesticides reduces sperm count and causes sperm damage in men. Women experience problems with their menstrual cycles, decreased fertility, and miscarriage. The general population of the United States has experienced a decline in fertility in all age groups, but it appears most sharply in women under age 25. Experiments on laboratory animals support the contention that environmental toxins are the cause. Increasing problems with the male reproductive system, including a rise in testicular cancer, may also be attributed to exposure to endocrine disruptors, possibly *in utero* (in the uterus) or very early in life.

A startling finding, published in 2005 in *Environmental Health Perspectives*, tracked the ratio of boys and girls born in an indigenous community living adjacent to a heavily polluted massive industrial complex in Canada. Before 1993, the sex ratio was normal, with slightly more than 50% boys. Between 1993 and 1999, the ratio of boys to girls began to drop, and by 2003 fewer than 35% of newborns were boys. This study did not identify the cause, and indeed there may be more than one, but chemicals and related factors that are associated with declining percentages of newborn boys include **dioxin**, PCBs, methyl mercury, maternal exposure to a pharmaceutical used in infertility treatment (clomiphene citrate) and parental smoking. The first three compounds will be discussed in Chapter 7 and Chapter 8.

WRAP-UP

Some 70,000 different chemical substances are in regular use throughout the world, and every year an estimated 1,000 new compounds are introduced. Pollutants are everywhere in the aquatic environment. Recent studies show that marine mammals contain 265 organic chemicals and 50 inorganic chemicals, up from 5 organic chemicals (in addition to mercury) in the 1960s. Chances are that freshwater organisms and humans contain a similar assortment of possible toxins. No one knows the effects of most of these pollutants. Because these chemicals have been proliferating only since the 1940s, it is possible to say that, in essence, the parents and grandparents alive today are experimenting on themselves and their children. Babies born today are exposed to thousands of chemicals simultaneously, starting at conception, with exposure to sperm and egg coming even sooner than that. Some of these chemicals are known to have deleterious effects individually, in lab experiments in cells or in animals, but many have not even been studied. Of those chemicals where the effects are known, the damage may be greatly underestimated because the harm done by a single chemical may be much less than the harm done by that chemical in a mixture. The combined effects of chemical pollutants and other environmental stresses are also unknown.

Toxic Organic Pollutants

This chapter discusses toxic organic pollutants—oil and gasoline, plastics, and organic chemicals. While these compounds are biodegradable, they may take a very long time to break down. Although fossil fuels are natural substances, they are harmful when burned or introduced into the environment. Plastics are harmful when proper procedures are not followed during their manufacture or disposal. Both fossil fuels and plastics contain chemicals that may be toxic to the environment. Toxic organic chemicals are used as gasoline additives, pesticides, insecticides, solvents, and flame retardants and can cause cancer, endocrine disruption, and many other illnesses to people and animals. The effects of many individual chemicals are not known, and even less is known about the effects of multiple chemicals.

OIL, GASOLINE, AND GASOLINE ADDITIVES

Oil and gasoline leak into inland waters from tankers, from pipelines, and from recreational watercraft. As happens in the oceans, pipelines and tankers can spill large amounts of oil into lakes and rivers. By far the largest source of oil in inland waters is the day-to-day runoff from roadways and other land surfaces. About 16 million gallons of oil are carried by rivers and streams into North American coastal waters each year. Runoff also contains the breakdown products of oil. Polynuclear aromatic hydrocarbons (PAHs), for example, are toxic to organisms even in very small doses.

Gasoline additives may also be pollutants. Beginning in 1992, in an effort to reduce air pollution from gasoline combustion, the U.S. government mandated the inclusion of oxygenate additives to gasoline. These compounds add oxygen to the gasoline, allowing it to burn more completely and, thus, more cleanly. The oil companies chose to use methyl tertiary butyl ether (MTBE) because it was less expensive than other suitable compounds. Although the chemical did reduce air pollutant emissions, in 1998 it was found be a potential human carcinogen (upgraded to "likely" by the EPA in 2005). The results of MTBE pollution are discussed in Chapter 11.

Benzene is an organic chemical emitted when some organic materials are incompletely burned. This chemical is produced by volcanoes, forest fires, and the combustion of crude oil and gasoline. Benzene is also found in cigarette smoke. Prior to the 1920s, benzene was used as an industrial solvent, but it was replaced by other solvents when it was discovered to be toxic. Benzene has sometimes been used as a gasoline additive. By far, the largest use for benzene today is in the manufacture of plastics, detergents, pesticides, and other chemicals, where it is synthesized from other petroleum compounds.

Benzene is a known carcinogen: Long-term exposure to high levels of it has been found to cause leukemia, particularly in children. Chronic exposure damages bone marrow and blood, depresses the immune system, and causes excessive bleeding. Benzene may be an endocrine disruptor because studies have shown that women who breathed high levels of it for many months showed a decrease in the size of their ovaries. Short-term exposure to high levels of benzene can cause drowsiness, dizziness, unconsciousness, or death.

PLASTIC

Plastics have been mass-produced for less than 50 years, but they are found everywhere. About 250 billion pounds (113 million metric tons) of plastics are produced each year. Plastic is the most common type of trash. It is found everywhere in and near inland waters, as litter tossed by inconsiderate passersby or deliberately dumped by municipalities and industries. Plastics may mar the locations where they are discarded, or they may be carried downstream by rivers or along the shore or across the water by lake currents, tainting even remote beaches far from where they were used.

Plastic is virtually indestructible. Although some of it is biodegradable, it takes about 400 years to decompose. Plastic waste is ingested by organisms that mistake it for food. Plastic pieces such as six-pack rings can bind a bird's beak shut or wrap around a seabird's neck, choking it.

The basic building block of polycarbonate plastic—used in making bottles, computer and electronics shells, CDs, crash helmets, and many other consumer products—is the compound bisphenol A (BPA). Invertebrates are sensitive to BPA, which causes deformed genitals in both sexes or superfeminization in females (excessive growth of female glands so that they rupture, causing the animal to die). Male fish downstream from a wastewater plant on the river Aire in England, with high levels of BPA, were found to be feminized: They had smaller testes and eggs within their testes. Sex reversals and altered sex organs in reptiles and malformed bird embryos have also been seen in the wild. Lab animals exposed to BPA have shown decreased fertility and the proliferation of breast cancer cells.

Plasticizers are substances that are used in plastics to impart viscosity, flexibility, and softness to a plastic product. About 90% of plasticizers are used for polyvinyl chloride (PVC), a popular plastic product used in diverse applications such as coatings, plumbing, construction materials, and plastic bottles. The most common plasticizers are the phthalates, which are classified as toxic chemicals by the EPA. About one billion pounds (450,000 metric tons) of phthalates are produced worldwide annually. Low doses of some phthalates *in utero* produce dramatic changes in sexual characteristics in laboratory animals. One recent study linked fetal exposure to phthalates with adverse effects on the human male reproductive system. These effects included hypospadias, a birth defect in which the opening of the penis is somewhere along the shaft rather than at the head, smaller penis size, incomplete testicular descent, and a small and indistinct scrotum. Other studies linked phthalate concentrations to lower sperm counts, reduced sperm motility, and more deformed sperm in men and premature breast development in girls.

PERSISTENT ORGANIC POLLUTANTS (POPS)

Man-made organic compounds contained in pesticides, flame retardants, industrial solvents, and cleaning fluids are commonly found in aquatic environments. Although these **persistent organic pollutants (POPs)** have many uses, some are toxic even in tiny amounts. According to a 2006 report by the World Health Organization (WHO), these toxic pollutants kill at least five million children a year. POPs do not biodegrade or dissipate in the environment. Environmental concerns have caused some to be banned. The table on pages 94 and 95 lists some of the hazardous POPs that are of most concern globally.

POPs are extremely effective at bioaccumulation. Animals eat tissues and shells with adsorbed POPs as they descend through the water column or after they accumulate in bottom sediments. As a result, concentrations are especially high in top predators that consume aquatic organisms. Examples of these predators include mammals such as otters, whales, and dolphins, and fish-eating birds such as eagles, ospreys, and gulls. One compound was found to be 71 times more concentrated in polar bears than in the seals they eat. Many POPs are toxic, some even in small amounts.

POPs evaporate and enter the atmosphere, particularly in warm conditions. Once in the air, they travel everywhere, even thousands of miles (km) from where they were used. The compounds then rain out of the atmosphere or attach to dust particles and are blown into lakes and streams. POPs are found in high levels even in animals and people that inhabit the remote reaches of the planet. Researchers in the 1980s were shocked to discover that the breast milk of native women in the Canadian Arctic, which they analyzed because they needed a control and assumed POP quantities would be minimal, had high concentrations of these toxins.

Most POPs are insoluble in water but are soluble in fats. Polar bears rely on stored body fat for part of the year, making them particularly vulnerable to the effects of POPs. People, too, metabolize the chemicals when they lose weight or pass nutrients on to a developing fetus or in breast milk.

One POP with an infamous history is the insecticide DDT. First used in 1939, the chemical was thought to be ideal—cheap, persistent in the environment, extremely toxic to insects on contact but less so to other animals—and seemingly safe for humans. In its early years, DDT did good work: It helped to prevent typhus in Europe during and after World War II, control malaria and other insect-borne diseases in tropical and subtropical areas, and reduce pests in developed nations.

Over time, however, it was discovered that DDT breaks down into extremely harmful compounds. When these compounds bioaccumulate in female birds, they disrupt the endocrine system and interfere with the manufacture of calcium. The birds lay eggs with extremely thin shells that break when the mother birds sit on them. Peregrine falcons, eagles, barn owls, and kingfishers were just a few of the birds whose populations plummeted as a result of widespread DDT use. The public outcry instigated by Rachel Carson's momentous 1962 book, *Silent Spring*, led to DDT's ban in the United States in 1973.

Besides the damage DDT causes to wildlife, the Environmental Protection Agency lists the chemical as a likely carcinogen. The insecticide has been linked to a reduction in the duration of lactation, meaning that new mothers exposed to DDT are able to produce breast milk for a shorter period of time than those who are not exposed.

DDT has been banned in most countries and has been replaced by other pesticides with no negative effects. But that has not been the case in some tropical areas where malaria is rampant: As DDT use

Some Synthetic Organic Chemicals Found in Freshwater

CHEMICAL	USE	AVAILABILITY	EFFECTS ON ANIMALS	EFFECTS ON HUMANS
Atrazine	Herbicide	Restricted use	In animal studies, causes damage to liver, kidney, and heart; causes tremors and changes organ weights; young wild frogs grow extra limbs or limbs in the wrong places; bioaccumulates	Possible carcinogen
Chlordane	Pesticide	Banned in United States	Has behavioral effects and causes liver cancer in lab animals; bioaccumulates	Possible carcinogen; damages liver and central nervous system, irritates eyes, skin; may cause nausea, blurred vision, convulsions
DDT*	Pesticide	Banned in much of the world	Endocrine disruptor; causes birds to lay eggs with thin shells	Probable carcinogen; shortens the duration of lactation (breast milk production)
Heptachlor*	Insecticide	Banned in the United States	Causes cancer in lab animals; causes damage to liver and chromosomes	Possible carcinogen; toxic to children; in fetuses and infants, associated with stillbirths and immune system and nervous system disorders
Hexachloro-benzene*	Fungicide, industrial chemical, byproduct	Regulated	Causes cancer in lab animals and damage to liver, kidneys, and ovaries; bioaccumulates in fish and animal tissues	Probable human carcinogen; causes liver disease; contact to skin causes severe light sensitivity

	Type	Status	Effects on wildlife/animals	Effects on humans
Toxaphene*	Pesticide	Banned in United States	Causes cancer in lab animals; bioconcentrates in aquatic organisms	High levels damage lungs, liver, kidneys, and nervous system or cause death; likely human carcinogen; an irritant when absorbed through skin or eyes
Trichloroethylene	Industrial solvent	Being phased out	Causes liver cancer in mice but not rats; same discrepancy on reproductive effects	Weak association with cancer; may work with other chemicals to be a carcinogen
Polychlorinated biphenyls (PCBs)*	Industrial chemical	Banned in the United States	Carcinogen in lab animals; linked to deformities in wildlife and commonly detected in tissues and eggs of fish-eating birds.	Very toxic mixture that affects skin, liver, nervous system, digestive tract; likely human carcinogen
Dioxins*	Byproduct; created in manufacture of PVC, among other products		Highly toxic and strong carcinogen in animals; rapidly bioaccumulates in fatty tissues of aquatic organisms	Known to cause skin problems, liver damage, gastric ulcers, severe weight loss, reproductive problems; stored in liver and fat

Source: Environmental Protection Agency

* One of the "Dirty Dozen" chemicals being regulated under the Convention on Persistent Organic Pollutants. Some of the Dirty Dozen chemicals not included in the table are the pesticides aldrin, dieldrin, endrin, mirex, and the industrial byproducts furans.

has declined, the incidence of malaria has increased tremendously. After weighing the costs and benefits of this situation, the international community is allowing the limited use of DDT in countries where malaria is prevalent.

Polychlorinated biphenyls (PCBs) are extremely stable, water-soluble compounds that were once used as flame retardants; to cool and insulate electrical devices; to manufacture paints, plastics, adhesives, and other materials; and to strengthen wood and concrete. PCBs were never supposed to be released into the environment, but they leaked from equipment and waste disposal sites. Their stability allows them to remain in the soil and water for many years. Although PCBs have been

Rachel Carson: *Founder of the Modern Environmental Movement*

Rachel Carson (1907–1964) grew up with a love of nature. Born in a small Pennsylvania river town, she became well known through her articles and books on the natural history of the oceans, including her prize-winning 1951 book *The Sea Around Us* and her 1955 book *The Edge of the Sea*. However, Carson is best remembered for her final book, *Silent Spring*. In the late 1950s, the biologist became alarmed as she observed the effects of chemical pesticides on the natural environment. She noted that since the mid-1940s, over 200 chemicals had been developed for killing insects, weeds, rodents, and other "pests," and these chemicals were blanketing the country. *Silent Spring*, published in 1962, was a best seller. The book warned readers about the long-term consequences of the "indiscriminate use" of pesticides:

The sprays, dusts and aerosols are now applied almost universally to farms, gardens, forests and homes—non-selective chemicals that have the power to kill every insect, the good and the bad, to still the song of birds and the leaping of fish in the streams—to coat the leaves with a deadly film and to linger on in soil—all this, though the intended target may be only a few weeds or insects. Can anyone believe it is possible to lay down such a barrage of poisons on the surface of the earth without making it unfit for all life?

banned in industrialized nations for decades, they are still everywhere in the environment, particularly in the animals at the top of the food web. Fortunately, concentrations of PCBs are dropping as they become attached to sediments, fall to lake bottoms, and are buried. Still, in some larger freshwater lakes, such as Lake Superior, they are consumed by small invertebrates, which are eaten by bottom-dwelling sport fish, which become part of the meals of fishers and their families.

The damage wrought by PCBs is multifaceted. They are extremely toxic to fish and invertebrates, even in small concentrations, and are strong endocrine disruptors. They interfere with reproduction and development in birds and mammals, reducing the number and survival rates of their offspring. In mammals, PCBs interfere with the

Silent Spring had a tremendous impact. People all around the country—including those in town meetings, members of Congress, and even President John F. Kennedy—began to talk about the damaging effects of chemical pesticides. As a result of Carson's book, President Kennedy's Science Advisory Committee issued a pesticide report in 1963 urging that chemical pesticides be used judiciously and called for more research into their health effects.

While alerting people to the hazards of indiscriminate pesticide use, Carson also tried to change the public's view of nature. In a 1963 segment about her work on the television show *CBS Reports*, Carson said:

We still talk in terms of conquest. We still haven't become mature enough to think of ourselves as only a tiny part of a vast and incredible universe. Man's attitude is today critically important simply because we have now acquired a fateful power to alter and destroy nature. But man is a part of nature, and his war against nature is inevitably a war against himself.

Carson continued to spread her message, even testifying before Congress in 1963 while suffering from breast cancer. She died of the disease at age 56, in 1964. While John Muir had shown the power of people to preserve wild places, Rachel Carson took the environmental movement a step further. She empowered the public to be aware of and have a say in human activities that alter the health of their environment.

metabolism of thyroid hormones, which regulate a diversity of physiological processes, including brain development and metabolism. PCBs also reduce immune system function: Polar bears are losing their ability to fight common infections and are also beginning to show some endocrine effects, such as masculinization in some females. According to a 2007 report published in the *Proceedings of the National Academy of Sciences*, newborn rats exposed to PCBs before birth and from their mother's milk showed damage to their auditory cortex, the part of the brain that is impaired in autistic children.

In humans, PCB exposure has been linked to developmental neurological problems in children, liver dysfunction, skin and respiratory problems, dizziness, and possibly cancer. One recent study found that levels of three chemicals (PCBs, hexachlorobenzene, and chlordane) were higher in the mothers of men with testicular cancer than in a control group, suggesting that the cancer was initiated in utero.

Since May 2004, POPs have been regulated under the Convention on Persistent Organic Pollutants. With this treaty, ratifying nations have agreed to reduce or eliminate the production or release of the "Dirty Dozen" of synthetic chemicals, some of which are listed in the table on pages 94 and 95. These nations are also working to identify other POPs that should be added to the list. Among the new substances under consideration are the flame retardants penta-BDE and hexa-BB; the pesticide chlordecone; and hexachlorohexane (HCH), which is the active ingredient in the pesticide lindane, a substance that is used to treat head lice. By the terms of the convention, DDT will continue to be used but will be limited to preventing the spread of malaria. The treaty has been ratified by the European Community, the United Kingdom, and many developing nations. The United States has not ratified the treaty, although most of the chemicals listed so far are already banned.

MULTIPLE CHEMICALS COMBINED

Scientists ordinarily study the effects of potentially toxic chemicals separately and in high concentrations, but in nature these chemicals are often found in tiny amounts and combined with others. Research on the effects on wildlife of low doses of multiple chemicals combined is just beginning. In a 2006 study led by Professor Tyrone Hayes at the University of California, Berkeley, and published in the journal *Environmental Health Perspectives*, tadpoles were exposed to mixtures of pesticides at concentrations of 0.1 ppb or 10 ppb. (Most of these pesticides were only known previously from studies in which they were administered at levels at least 10,000 times higher.) In this study, the mortality rate of tadpoles exposed to individual pesticides at 0.1 ppb ranged from 0% to 7.8%, depending on the pesticides. When the nine pesticides were mixed with each at 0.1 ppb, 35% of the tadpoles died. Those that lived to metamorphosis took a longer time to metamorphose, were smaller than other frogs after metamorphosis, and experienced neurological damage, deformities, or increased susceptibility to diseases. These animals also had four times the amount of stress hormone in their blood as animals in the control group. When the nine pesticides were mixed with each at 10 ppb, all of the tadpoles died.

WRAP-UP

There are not yet comprehensive or effective regulations to deal with toxic organic pollutants, either nationally or internationally. Even the Convention on Persistent Organic Pollutants regulates only 12 (with a few more to be added) of the most toxic chemicals out of the hundreds of potentially hazardous compounds. A ban can be put into effect only if politicians, who are usually not trained in biology or chemistry, decide that the costs of a chemical outweigh its benefits; but this is likely to happen only after the substance has been in use for years or decades and is pervasive in the environment.

8

Toxic Inorganic Pollutants

This chapter discusses toxic inorganic pollutants—acids, salts, and heavy metals that are not biodegradable, although they may become diluted or break down chemically. Acids are created in the atmosphere and form acid rain, which is particularly damaging to aquatic environments. This chapter will also describe how acid rain forms and the consequences it has on aquatic environments. (Strategies for decreasing acid rain formation and mitigating its effects are described in Chapter 11.) Pharmaceuticals are designed to initiate a physiological response in people or animals and may do so in organisms unintentionally when they are released into the environment. Sediments and heat in unnatural amounts also act as pollutants.

ACID POLLUTION

Pollutants and water vapor combine in the atmosphere to form acids, which fall as acid rain or other acid precipitation. Acid rain does its major damage in waterways and forests, where it strips the soil of its nutrients and metals. The acids and metals are transported into ponds, where they can damage freshwater ecosystems. Large amounts of acid alter a pond or lake ecosystem and, in some cases, may completely destroy it.

Acid Rain

Natural rainfall is slightly acidic, with a pH of about 5.6. Rain's acidity is due to the small amount of carbon dioxide that dissolves in the water droplets to form mild carbonic acid. Acid rain is more acidic than normal, with a pH of less than 5.0.

Several steps lead to the creation of acid rain. Sulfur dioxide (SO_2) and the nitrogen oxides (NO_2 and NO, which together are symbolized by NO_x) are released into the atmosphere primarily by coal-burning power plants or from metal ore refineries. These oxide gases then react with water vapor to produce sulfuric acid and nitric and nitrous acid. The acids dissolve in water droplets, which combine as normal droplets do to form raindrops—in this case, acid raindrops.

Sulfuric and nitric acids are strong acids. Rainwater in the northeastern United States, with a pH typically between 4.0 and 4.5, is ten times more acidic than natural rain. This region is afflicted with acid precipitation due to the high density of medium- and large-sized industrial cities, such as Pittsburgh; the highly populated area that runs from Washington, D.C., north to Boston; and the concentration of power and industrial plants in West Virginia and other locales. In addition to the acid-producing pollutants generated locally, additional acids are blown in from factories and power plants in the Midwest.

Sulfur and nitrogen oxides released from tall smokestacks may drift as far as 600 miles (1,000 km) downwind: Therefore, acid rain problems in one area may originate far away. This situation has strained relations between states and countries. For example, in the Scandinavian countries, acid rain is an environmental crisis. All of Sweden's rainfall in 2000 had a pH of less than 5.05. Yet, the acid-producing emissions that caused the acidity came from factories in the United Kingdom and Western Europe. Fortunately, these countries have

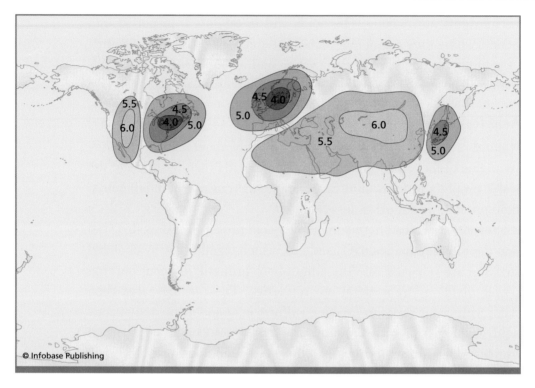

Global pH values of rainfall show high acidity over eastern North America, western Europe, and southeast Asia.

decreased their emissions by 70% from their maximum high, and the natural acid balance is slowly returning in Scandinavia. Canada's acid rain problem originates largely in the factories and power plants of the United States. In 1998, the United States produced more than 6 times the SO_2 emissions and 11 times the NO_x emissions of Canada. Emissions decreases of 40% in the United States have begun to be felt in Canada. Still, according to the United Nations Environmental Programme, acid rain remains a problem over large parts of North America and Europe and is becoming a major issue in Southeast Asia, where emissions are growing precipitously. Some creative methods for reducing sulfur and nitrogen oxides have been developed and will be described in Chapter 11.

The Effects of Acid Rain on Lakes and Streams

The type of the rock and soil in a specific locality helps explain why acid rain can cause great damage in some regions and cause little damage in others. Rocks and soils that contain calcium carbonate, including limestone, marble, and their soils, can neutralize an acidic solution, a quality called buffering capacity. The pH of ponds and streams situated in these rock types will be nearly normal, even if the rainwater is acidic. Nebraska, Indiana, and other midwestern states do not suffer from acid rain problems due to their well-buffered soils. However, if the buffering capacity of these rocks and soils is exceeded, the region will be vulnerable to acid damage. Most rock and soil, including the metamorphic rocks of the northeastern United States, have little buffering capacity. Where buffering capacity is low and rainfall is acidic, some soils have increased their acid levels by five- to ten-fold in the past few decades.

Acidic soils lower the pH of the streams that flow over them. According to an Environmental Protection Agency (EPA) report in 2000, approximately 580 of the streams in the Mid-Atlantic Coastal Plain were found to be acidic, including 90% of streams in the Pine Barrens of New Jersey—the highest percentage in the nation. Acidic streams add more acidity to lakes, ponds, and marshes, increasing the acidity already brought into those water bodies by acid rain. This combined acidity has lowered the pH of some lakes in the Northeastern United States to below 5.0. For example, Little Echo Pond in Franklin, New York, has a pH of 4.2. The Canadian government estimates that 14,000 lakes in eastern Canada are acidic.

Another problem occurs as acid rainwater filters through the soil. The acid invades the soil's minerals and replaces the ions that serve as good plant nutrients—such as calcium, magnesium, and potassium—with hydrogen ions from the acid. The freed nutrients then wash away in the runoff, so that the soil can no longer nourish the plants. Acidic waters also leach metals such as aluminum from the soil and transport them to freshwater lakes, ponds, and streams. In areas where they accumulate in high enough concentrations, these metals become toxic to aquatic life.

The Effects of Acid Rain on Freshwater Ecosystems

Lakes and streams with low pH support a lower quantity and variety of life. Most aquatic plants grow best in water with a pH of 7.0 to 9.2. As pH decreases, plant numbers decline, which reduces food for some water birds. If pH continues to lower, the numbers of freshwater shrimp, crayfish, clams, and some fish start to dwindle. At pH 5.5, the bacteria that decompose leaf litter and other debris begin to die, cutting off the nutrient supply for plankton. If acid runoff brings aluminum into the lake in great quantities, fish populations experience additional stress, leading to lower body weight and smaller size. Native fish are then less able to compete with alien species for food and habitat.

As their environment becomes intolerable, fish populations decline. Young fish that hatch into acidic, metal-rich waters will not survive into adulthood, or they may be deformed or stunted in their growth. If the pH goes below 5, females will not spawn, and fish eggs will not hatch. These stresses make the fish more vulnerable to disease and other problems. With a pH below 5, adult fish die. Lake water with a pH less than 4.5 becomes entirely devoid of fish. In Sweden, 18,000 lakes are so acidic that all the fish have died. Loss of bacteria causes organic material to lie undecayed on the bottom of a lake while allowing moss to cover its shores.

Melting snow or heavy downpours can bring in excess acidic runoff, sharply and temporarily lowering the pH of streams and lakes. Waterways that already have low pH are at risk of serious damage from these temporary increases in acidity. Temporary acidification can completely upset an ecosystem and result in massive fish kills.

Although frogs can tolerate lower acidity than fish, they cannot live without food. Thus, the loss of food due to increased acidity of the water causes their populations to decline. Birds and mammals that depend on the lake for fish or plants also die off or leave the area. However, some organisms—plants and mosses, and black fly larvae—tolerate or even thrive in an acidic environment. In fact, acid rain can invert whole freshwater ecosystems, allowing lakes to be taken over by alien organisms and leaving few, if any, native organisms.

SALT

Salt is naturally found in aquatic environments in varying amounts, but it is a pollutant if the concentrations become too high for an individual body of water. The salt used to clear icy roadways in winter, predominantly sodium chloride (the same substance used as table salt), runs off into nearby streams and lakes. Salt concentrations in freshwater bodies are highest in places where there are more roads and harsh winters. In the heavily developed northeastern United States, some streams and lakes have chloride concentrations between 3 and 25 times more than normal. Even in rural areas with few roads, chloride amounts are higher than in water bodies with no nearby roads.

As development in the Northeast continues, more roads will require more salt that will, in turn, accumulate in the environment. Peter M. Groffman of the Institute of Ecosystem Studies in Millbrook, New York, predicts that many freshwater bodies may reach concentrations up to 100 times their normal concentration. If this occurs, the water will be undrinkable and also toxic to aquatic organisms, which will affect their growth and reproduction. At this time, salt is not regulated as a freshwater contaminant.

HEAVY METALS

Most heavy metals are a natural part of the environment in low concentrations. Iron and aluminum, for example, are important components of many types of rocks, and mercury and lead are spewed out by volcanoes. Plants and animals require tiny amounts of some heavy metals to carry out their life processes. Hemoglobin, the molecule that transports oxygen in the blood, utilizes iron. Many enzymes contain zinc. Other heavy metals required for life processes include copper, vanadium, and cobalt.

All heavy metals are toxic to organisms in some quantity. Mercury, lead, and cadmium are not used by plants or animals and are toxic even in minute quantities. Heavy metals that are biologically useful in small amounts are poisonous in larger quantities. Because these metals bioaccumulate, they are especially dangerous to animals that feed high on the food chain.

Human activities discharge heavy metals into the environment. Burning coal, fuel oils, fuel additives, and trash release heavy metals into the air, as does steel and iron manufacturing. The metals eventually fall or are rained out of the atmosphere. Runoff from the land brings heavy metals from atmospheric fallout, mines and metal refineries, urban areas, human waste, landfills, and contaminated sediments into inland waters. Large storms cleanse areas that may have been isolated. Storm waters are particularly laden with heavy metals.

Mercury is probably the most damaging heavy metal, and is most hazardous when released into the atmosphere by the combustion of coal. In addition, the burning of municipal and medical wastes discharges large quantities of mercury into the atmosphere. Once released, the metal cools and turns into aerosol droplets. These droplets may travel hundreds of miles through the atmosphere but will eventually fall to the ground or into the water to be deposited into sediment. Bacteria then convert this mercury into organic mercury, usually the dangerous methyl mercury.

Methyl mercury is easily absorbed through the skin, lungs, and gut of animals. The compound is extremely toxic and is poisonous to some algae and to the larvae of some small invertebrates. Methyl mercury bioaccumulates in top predators including fish, such as tuna, that people consume. Humans are very sensitive to methyl mercury: It causes brain, liver, and kidney damage. Recognition of the dangers of mercury to human health resulted in a great decrease in global mercury production beginning in 1990.

Enormous amounts of lead are produced each year, and it is the most common toxic material found in humans. In the form of tetraethyl lead, it has been used as a gasoline additive or as a component of paints. The metal is ubiquitous in computer screens, electronics, batteries, medical equipment, and a myriad of other modern devices. Lead enters the water in fallout from the atmosphere, in industrial waste, from landfills, and in gasoline residue. The metal is not toxic to lower organisms and does not seem to bioaccumulate. People obtain

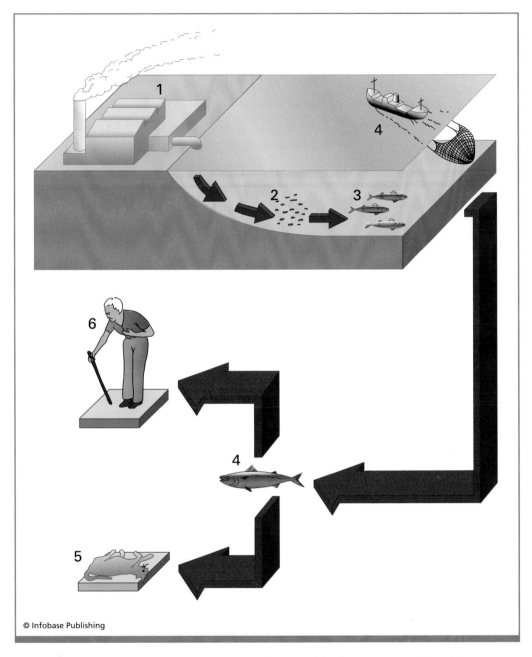

The inhabitants of Minamata, Japan, suffered irreparable damage to their health as a result of industrial mercury pollution. The first cases of Minamata disease—a severe and sometimes fatal affliction of the nervous system, were discovered in 1953. Since then, more than 1,200 deaths have been attributed to the disease.

most of their lead by breathing it from the atmosphere or by ingest-ing it in paint flakes. Lead leads to nervous system, brain, and blood disorders, especially in children. According to a 2006 World Health Organization report, each year, 18 million children around the world suffer neurological damage because of lead poisoning.

Tributyltin (TBT) is a stabilizer in plastics and a major ingredi-ent in antifouling paint. It is used on the hulls of oceangoing ships (which may enter freshwater rivers and lakes) to keep barnacles and other organisms from growing on them. Used in this way, the com-pound is extremely toxic to aquatic life. TBT is an endocrine disruptor at lower doses, causing severe reproductive effects in aquatic organ-isms. Exposed females of some species of freshwater snails (from the order Prosobranchia) grow penises or develop other forms of mascu-linization. In mammals, including humans, TBT brings about immune system decline. In higher doses, the compound causes neural, respi-ratory, and psychological disturbances, in addition to abdominal pain, vomiting and other problems.

PHARMACEUTICALS

Pharmaceutical pollutants include human and veterinary drugs, and even illicit (recreational) drugs. Synthetic hormones such as those in birth control pills are a major problem in the waterways, but they are not the only pharmaceuticals that find their way into the environment. The amount of pharmaceuticals and personal care products (sham-poos, suntan lotions, perfumes, and soaps, for example) that finds its way into the environment each year is equal to the amount of pesti-cides used annually.

Medications found in streams include antidepressants, hormones, cholesterol-lowering medications, and antibiotics. In an extensive study by the United States Geological Service (USGS) in 1999 and 2000, 139 streams around the United States were found to contain 46 pharmaceuticals. (The antidepressant drug Prozac was found in 28 of 44 streams.) These findings are not restricted to the United

States: Sewage effluent from a plant in Germany sampled in 2000 contained 36 drugs and five drug **metabolites** (the remainder of a compound, such as a drug, that has been altered by passage through the human body).

Wildlife is feeling the effects of these medications. Antidepressants have been seen to alter sperm levels and the spawning patterns of fish. At Gettysburg College in Pennsylvania, in 1998, Dr. Peter Fong added low levels of Prozac to tanks containing mussels and clams. This caused the animals to release their eggs and sperm too early. In the wild, this would likely result in no offspring. Prozac may be partly responsible for the decline seen in amphibian populations. In laboratory experiments published in a 2004 study, fertilized frog eggs were placed in tanks with the same concentrations of fluoxetine (the active ingredient in Prozac) found in a river in Mississippi. Over 166 days, 40% of the eggs died, compared with only 16% of those in clean water. Those animals that survived were about 40% smaller than normal and were also disoriented. Of course, an animal that cannot tell which way to swim when confronted by a predator is unlikely to survive.

Other drugs are found in waterways as well. Antibiotics (and antibiotic soaps) are created to kill bacteria. Yet many species of bacteria are beneficial to the environment, and antibiotics are not always selective about which bacteria they kill. Bacteria have been known to develop resistance to antibiotics, and even low-level concentrations of these substances in the environment could increase the number of disease-causing bacteria that are able to resist these medications.

Proper disposal of pharmaceutical waste is a complex issue, and consistent guidelines are not yet in place. Because pharmaceuticals are not regulated as pollutants, people in households can dispose of them however they choose, although medical-care facilities do have guidelines for the disposal of unused pharmaceuticals.

At this time, sewage treatment plants are not required to eliminate medications, although the EPA is studying whether this should change. Cost estimates for better filtration are around $100 million for each large sewage treatment plant. Because the money would come from municipalities, it would be subtracted from the budgets of other public services such as schools and hospitals.

SEDIMENTS

The runoff of clay, silt, and sand from the land into streams and lakes is a natural and necessary process. Sediments build up floodplains and wetlands, and they bring nutrients with them. However, logging, plowing, and other disturbances to the land caused by the construction of roads or buildings can cause excess sediment runoff.

Sediments become pollutants if they muddy a stream or lake and hinder photosynthesis, bury aquatic ecosystems, and clog the feeding apparatus or gills of animals. Also, sediments may have toxic chemicals attached to them, thus providing the chemicals with a mode of transportation through the ecosystem.

THERMAL POLLUTION

Just as a car engine becomes hot as it converts fuel to usable energy, power plants and industrial plants generate waste heat. These plants are usually located on waterways because the least expensive way to dissipate waste heat is to use water from a river, lake, or the ocean. **Thermal pollution** is the introduction of this waste heat into the environment.

To cool a plant, water is drawn from the waterway, routed through the area that needs to be cooled, and then returned to the waterway. Estimates are that almost half of all water used in the United States each year is for cooling electric power plants. A 1,000-megawatt power plant heats more than 2 million gallons (10 million l) of water by 95°F (35°C) every hour. The water surrounding a plant may be as much as 18°F (10°C) higher than the water farther away.

Heated water has multiple effects on the nearby ecosystem. Warmer temperatures increase the ability of plants to photosynthesize, which may spur an algal bloom. Warmer temperatures also increase the stress on plants and animals in the water. Warm water holds less dissolved oxygen than cool water, making it more difficult for aquatic animals to breathe. Some species suffocate in water temperatures greater than 95°F (35°C). Higher temperatures and lower oxygen may increase the animals' susceptibility to problems from pathogens and toxic chemicals. As a result, the **biodiversity**—the number of different species in the ecosystem—may decrease. Studies have shown that phytoplankton diversity decreases at thermal waste sites.

Temperature changes may harm fish and other aquatic organisms in other ways. Fish and invertebrates are **ectotherms**: Their body temperatures are the same as the surrounding water. These "cold-blooded" animals are slow moving and slow growing and are adapted to a specific water temperature. Warmer temperatures speed their metabolism; for example, their heart rate doubles with every 18°F (10°C) rise in water temperature, which harms their ability to survive and reproduce. Native fish that like cooler water, such as trout, may lose ground while nonnative species, algae, and bacteria may increase and thrive. (By contrast, **endotherms** are "warm-blooded" animals that keep their body temperatures nearly constant, independent of the temperature of their surroundings. Endotherms fuel their warmth by eating a lot of food and maintain their body temperatures with insulation such as fur, feathers, and blubber.)

Power plants have different types of cooling systems. The easiest and cheapest cooling method is the once-through system described on page 110. Cool water is withdrawn from a nearby water body, and hot water is returned to the same water body. The once-through system is by far the most environmentally destructive. Closed-cycle cooling reuses the cooling water so that the waste heat does not leave the plant. A favored type of closed-cycle cooling, which is expensive to build and operate, pumps the hot water into towers, where the excess heat is released into the atmosphere.

New York's Hudson River has five power plants (four fossil-fuel and one nuclear) that use the once-through system. At peak use, they altogether draw 5 billion gallons (19 million l) of water a day. The nuclear power plant at Indian Point, the largest of the five, uses nearly twice as much water as New York City and Westchester County combined. Two-thirds of the energy produced by the plant becomes not electricity, but unusable heat. Plants, eggs, larvae, and juvenile fish, including about 35% of the young striped bass in that portion of the river, are lost as the cooling water runs through the plant. Some larger fish are killed or injured when they are trapped on the screens that prevent them from being sucked into the cooling system. In contrast, closed-cycle technology not only drastically limits waste heat, it also reduces fish kills by up to 97%.

Though less dramatic and voluminous, thermal pollution that enters the water as runoff from paved surfaces is an important problem. Because pavement absorbs heat better than natural surfaces, especially in the summer, the temperature of water flowing from a parking lot may be a few degrees higher than water flowing off a natural surface. Even small differences in temperature can alter the environment enough to stress the native fish and plant species.

STREAM STUDIES

Until recently, the technology to measure potentially toxic chemicals at extremely low concentrations did not exist. Recent measurements now show shocking amounts and varieties of chemicals in water, animals, and people. In the United States, more than 700 chemicals have been detected in drinking water, 129 of them considered highly toxic. In the most extensive study to date, 139 streams were sampled by the USGS in 1999 and 2000 in search of 95 organic wastewater contaminants. These pollutants were selected because they are used in significant quantities, are found in wastewater, have raised concerns about their health or environmental safety, are representative of certain classes of compounds, and can be accurately measured. The compounds, which included 33 known or suspected endocrine disruptors, are just a small subset of potentially harmful chemicals that are being used by society. The streams in the study were chosen because they are known to be contaminated, and they are not considered representative of all streams in the country. According to Dana Klopin, USGS research hydrologist and first author on the study, the most contaminated streams contained the largest percentage of sewage effluent. Water from 80% of the streams studied contained one or more of the compounds; one stream had 38 compounds.

Of the 95 compounds tested for, 82 were found in at least one sample, mostly in very low concentrations. All of the potential endocrine disruptors were detected in at least one stream. Three groups of compounds (detergent metabolites, plasticizers, and steroids) accounted for 80% of the total contaminants. Concentrations of nonprescription drugs were also very high. Some compounds were present in smaller amounts than expected because they adhere to sediments. Only the compounds in question were analyzed in the study. Some of them may be degrading into new, more persistent compounds and be present in the environment in a form that was not detected.

WRAP-UP

Waterways in the developed nations, and, increasingly, in the developing nations, are a microcosm of all of the compounds people use for agriculture or industry, for power generation, and for health and beauty. Altogether, streams have been found to contain every potentially hazardous compound that scientists have looked for so far, and most streams contain more than one. The worst off are those bodies of water that receive a lot of effluent from wastewater treatment plants or industry. Not all of these pollutants are filtered out before the water is used for drinking, and they cause damage to aquatic environments and organisms.

Biological Pollutants

This chapter will discuss biological pollutants: living organisms that are more abundant than they should be in a particular location, or that are found in places where they do not belong. Although nutrients are not organisms, they are included in this chapter because when they are present in excess, they encourage the rampant growth of aquatic plants, throwing a waterway's ecosystem out of balance. Invasive species are introduced to an ecosystem that contains no predators: If conditions are favorable, these invasives drive out the native species. Pathogens are part of the natural environment but are present in enormous numbers where people live closely together and the water they use is polluted by both human and animal waste. The most common diseases in the developing world are related to unclean water.

NUTRIENTS

Nutrients enter streams and lakes from runoff from land, fallout from the atmosphere, and recycling of plant and animal tissue within the aquatic environment. Without nutrients, plants and animals could not grow, replenish their bodies, or have energy for living. Because they are essential for life, it seems impossible that nutrients could be a pollutant, yet nutrients are the most serious pollutants entering fresh-water systems today. Recent escalations in nutrient input are having a dire effect on freshwater ecosystems.

Nutrients themselves are sometimes toxic. Depending on temperature and pH, ammonia can be poisonous to fish and other aquatic organisms. Excess nutrients come primarily from human and animal wastes, detergents, and fertilizers. Sewage and runoff that enters the water directly, either from a deliberate act or from leaks and spills from wastewater lagoons, carry an enormous amount of nutrient pollution. If the nutrient load is extreme, fish die. In 2000, Cargill Pork, Inc., dumped hog waste into the Loutre River in Missouri, killing 53,000 fish. In 2005, at a mega-dairy in New York State, manure and other wastes blew out the wall of an earthen-walled reservoir that held 3 million gallons (11 million l) of manure, enough to fill six Olympic-size swimming pools. The waste flowed into the Black River, a popular fishing stream and a water source for downstream towns, triggering a major fish kill and the temporary shutdown of all recreation on the river.

Although this did not occur in any of the incidents mentioned, high nitrate concentrations in drinking water can result in the condition in infants known as methemoglobinemia or "blue baby" syndrome. In this illness, the baby's digestive system converts the nitrates to nitrite, a process that interferes with the blood's ability to carry oxygen. The baby's tissues, deprived of oxygen, turn blue.

Smaller quantities of nutrients in a lake do not cause an immediate fish kill but accelerate **eutrophication**. Eutrophication is part of a lake's natural aging process as it progresses from oligotrophic to meso-trophic to eutrophic. Excess nutrients drastically reduce the natural pace of this process from thousands of years to just a few years.

During eutrophication, excess nutrients act as fertilizer for algae and acquatic plants and bring on what is called a *bloom*. When the plants die, bacteria populations expand to consume the tissue. These aerobic bacteria need oxygen, and an enormous number of them deplete the gas from the water. The decaying tissue also warms the

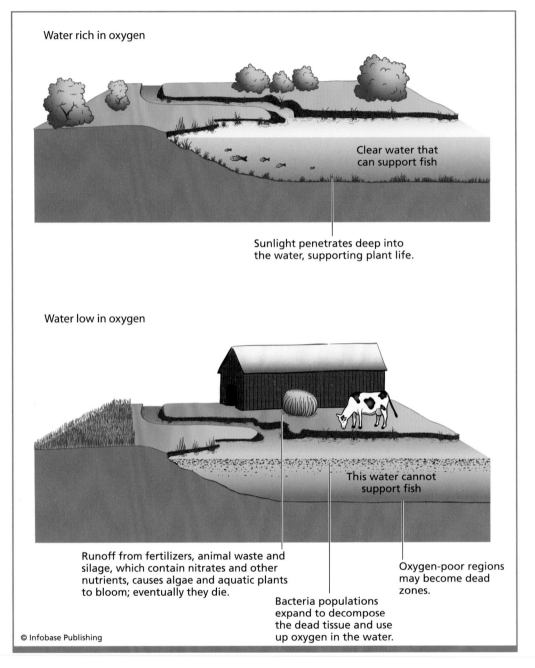

Water rich in oxygen

Clear water that
can support fish

Sunlight penetrates deep into
the water, supporting plant life.

Water low in oxygen

This water cannot
support fish

Runoff from fertilizers, animal waste and
silage, which contain nitrates and other
nutrients, causes algae and aquatic plants
to bloom; eventually they die.

Bacteria populations
expand to decompose
the dead tissue and use
up oxygen in the water.

Oxygen-poor regions
may become dead
zones.

© Infobase Publishing

Eutrophication occurs when a body of water accumulates very high concentrations
of nutrients. As a result, algae and plants flourish and consume nearly all of the
available oxygen. Much of the native wildlife perishes due to the lack of
life-supporting oxygen.

lake's water, causing oxygen and other gases to bubble out into the atmosphere. Oxygen-poor water is called **hypoxic**; fish and most other animals cannot survive in it. Hypoxic waters then become **dead zones**, regions that are hostile to most forms of life. As native species die off or leave the area, different species begin to appear.

The Black Sea has suffered severe eutrophication in recent decades, primarily from fertilizer use along the many rivers that drain into the basin. During the 1970s and 1980s, algal blooms became so intense that sunlight was blocked, and sea grasses could not photosynthesize. The high population of algae and the lack of photosynthesis depleted oxygen in the sea. Initially, fishers experienced an increase in their catch at the edges of the growing dead zone as the animals attempted to flee. Shortly afterward, shellfish and bottom-dwelling fish populations almost completely collapsed. In four or five years, the natural ecosystem disappeared, and an invasive species of comb jellies took over. The comb jellies were so successful in the Black Sea that in a few years their combined weight exceeded the entire world's commercial fish catch, although they were then replaced by another invasive species of comb jelly. The Black Sea is now showing weak signs of recovery because the Eastern European countries whose rivers drain into it can no longer afford fertilizer, although favorable climatic conditions may also have played a role in the recovery.

Dead zones are also found in coastal areas where rivers bring nutrients into the sea. One of the largest and most persistent dead zones in U.S. coastal waters lies in the Gulf of Mexico, which provides the nation with 70% of its shrimp and two-thirds of its oysters annually. Although the zone varies in size and duration from year to year, over the past two decades it has appeared earlier and grown larger each year. The growth of the zone is not surprising because triple the amount of fertilizer now runs downstream than did in the period from the 1950s to the 1970s. Flood protection has also contributed to the nutrient problem. Before the protection efforts, floodwaters ran over riverbanks and dumped nutrients back into the ground. But now the nutrients stay in the river's currents and drain into the Gulf.

Eutrophication has reduced the oxygen content of this water to near zero, resulting in a massive fish kill. *(SuperStock, Inc. / SuperStock)*

The eutrophication in the Gulf of Mexico develops in spring and early summer. The Mississippi River drains 41% of the land surface of the United States, including the rich farmland of the Midwest. Spring rains wash excess fertilizers from the soil into the river. Surplus nutrients also come from animal manure, golf courses (which use five times the fertilizer concentration that farmers use), urban lawns (which use twice the fertilizer concentration), and water treatment plants. These are minor sources compared to cropland, though, because they cover much less area. The dead zone disappears when the autumn storms mix hypoxic waters with normal water.

Typically, oxygen contents in Gulf waters are about 6.3 parts per million (ppm). About 7 to 10 days after spring rains begin in the agricultural regions, the oxygen content in the dead zone decreases to only about 0.6 ppm. The most intense hypoxia usually is found between 30 and 60 feet (9 and 18 m) below the surface. So far, the fish and shellfish catch has not been greatly affected, but the situation that occurred in the Black Sea suggests that ecosystem collapse is possible.

Researchers suggest that a 40% to 45% annual cutback in nitrogen use in the Mississippi River drainage area would be necessary to decrease the dead zone to 3,000 square miles (5,000 square km). Some scientists suggest that even comparatively minor sources of nitrate should be regulated, including the nitrogen oxide pollution that comes from cars. Programs for nutrient reduction, such as cap-and-trade, are described in more detail in Chapter 11.

Nutrient levels entering the Gulf can be reduced by cutting back the runoff. Both planting crops that cover the ground year round

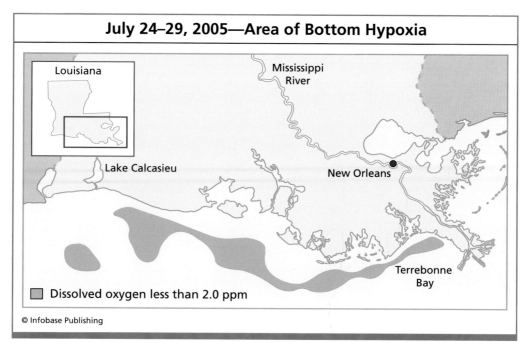

July 24–29, 2005—Area of Bottom Hypoxia

Louisiana

Mississippi River

Lake Calcasieu

New Orleans

Terrebonne Bay

☐ Dissolved oxygen less than 2.0 ppm

© Infobase Publishing

The Gulf of Mexico dead zone as surveyed on July 24 to 29, 2005. The shaded area depicts the portion of the Gulf in which dissolved oxygen content is less than 2.0 ppm.

rather than only part of the year and controlling drainage to keep more water in the ground will limit runoff. Preserving existing wetlands and creating new ones also reduce nutrient runoff because wetlands act as a buffer for pollutants. Farmers can create marshes around their fields and pump polluted water through the marshes to expose the nitrates to the bacteria that convert them to nitrogen gas. As a side benefit, such marshes are good environments for fish and water birds.

The history of the Gulf of Mexico dead zone mirrors that of the Black Sea. At this time, no one can predict how close the important Gulf fishery is to collapsing, although many researchers say that it is in danger. Eutrophication in the Gulf and elsewhere is a difficult problem to solve because the industries causing the problem are not the ones who are most affected by it.

INVASIVE SPECIES

Invasive species are an enormous problem in some areas, such as the Great Lakes. Over the past 200 years, the rate of species invasion has risen exponentially as people have moved more freely about the planet.

For an alien species, the main path to a new aquatic ecosystem is via ship. For instance, the ballast water drawn into tanks in ships to stabilize the vessels contains the organisms that happened to be swimming in the water when it was pumped in, such as plankton, jellies, larval mollusks, and crustaceans. When the ballast water is dumped, the nonnative species (often along with pollutants) are expelled with it. Species can also migrate to new environments while attached to boats and propellers. They can also travel packed with bait worms and other cargo.

Aquarium dumping is another common route for a nonnative species to invade a new water body. When people tire of their aquariums, or when their aquatic pets become problematic, they dump the organisms into the nearest stream, lake, or pond. Freshwater Asian clams (*Corbicula fluminea*), used in aquariums, are rapidly spreading and displacing native species in the United States. Thousands of water bodies are infested with aquarium plants that were dumped from tanks by their owners.

After a species is introduced to a new environment, several possible outcomes may result. In most circumstances, conditions for survival are not right, and the alien organism perishes. Sometimes, an alien species may be compatible with the natives and contribute to the biodiversity of the ecosystem. Rarely do invasive species thrive; but when they do, it may be because they have no predators and so are able to out-compete the native species for food and living space. Exploding populations of alien organisms greatly decrease the diversity of an ecosystem by altering the habitat to the degree that it becomes unsuitable for the native species, thereby driving the native species toward extinction.

The biggest disaster in the United States caused by an invasive species so far has been the spread of zebra mussels (*Dreissena polymorpha*). These voracious filter feeders are explosive reproducers, with females spewing out between 40,000 and 1 million eggs per season. Native to the Caspian Sea region, the tiny animals have spread throughout the Great Lakes system since they were first discovered, about two decades ago. The mollusks displace valuable native species and block water intake pipes, costing millions of dollars annually. The impact of zebra mussels in the Great Lakes is described in Chapter 12.

The costs of invasive species in the United States are estimated at $137 billion per year. Once a species establishes a foothold in the environment, it is difficult or impossible to stop it. The best approach is to prevent the invasion, yet a workable prevention program is difficult to figure out. Alan Burdick, in his 2005 book, *Out of Eden: An Odyssey of Ecological Invasion*, says, "Our current environmental legislation is poorly equipped to cope with this kind of invasion. Laws like the Endangered Species Act are intended to protect specific, known organisms from specific, known threats. Ecological invasion does not submit to such clarity."

The National Aquatic Invasive Species Act of 2007 provides money for research, to monitor and control new and existing threats, and to regulate ballast water. The act followed earlier acts that responded to the zebra mussel invasion. Burdick says, "Critics may carp about the cost—$836 million over several years—but that is a small fraction of the cost that the zebra mussel already exacts."

PATHOGENS

Water plays a role in about 80% of all infectious disease. Pathogens have always been present in the natural world, but human activity has increased their numbers and distribution. People living densely packed together, such as those in urban areas, are especially vulnerable to the spread of pathogenic illnesses. The more virulent a pathogen, the smaller the number of them it takes to establish an infection.

Pathogens and Waterborne Diseases

Pathogens can cause waterborne diseases directly. Thousands of people die of waterborne diseases each day, especially the very young, the very old, those with damaged immune systems, and those who are malnourished. Deaths occur almost entirely in developing countries, where diseases such as typhoid, cholera, and dysentery are rampant.

People who consume untreated or inadequately treated water are the most likely to ingest disease-causing pathogens. Waterborne diseases can lead to severe problems of the digestive system: Diarrhea is a common symptom of several of these diseases. The Centers for Disease Control (CDC) estimates that there are four billion cases of diarrhea globally each year, with two million of those being fatal. Diarrhea is the leading cause of childhood death, usually killing children under age five.

Even in developed nations, where water treatment plants are common, pathogens infect the water. Microbes may pass through sewage treatment plants that have been overwhelmed by flooding or may be resistant to treatment. More than half of the waterborne disease outbreaks in the United States are caused by chlorine-resistant microbes. One common waterborne disease is giardia, caused by drinking water containing a protozoan that spreads in animal feces, including those of dogs and beavers (resulting in its nickname, "beaver fever").

Another waterborne disease that strikes people living in the industrialized nations is **cryptosporidiosis**, caused by the single-celled microbe cryptosporidium. The parasite multiplies in the gut of mammals, birds, fish, and reptiles and is excreted through feces as an **oocyst** (the microbe's inactive form). Oocysts can persist in the environment for long periods under harsh conditions. Swallowing even a small amount of water infected with cryptosporidium oocysts can cause cryptosporidiosis. Cases of the illness increase when heavy rains wash through feedlots or when sewage treatment plants overload or break down. Because they are resistant to chlorine and other chemical disinfectants, oocysts can pass untreated through sewage treatment plants.

Symptoms of cryptosporidiosis include stomach cramps, vomiting, low-grade fever, and watery diarrhea. Symptoms usually appear four to six days after infection. Healthy people may be ill for several days but will recover on their own. However, infants, the elderly, and people with compromised immune systems, such as those undergoing

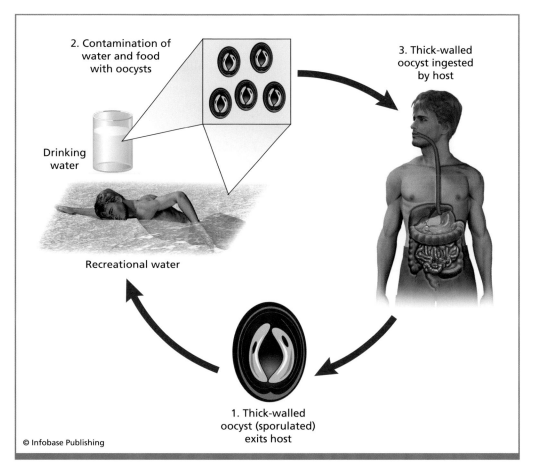

2. Contamination of water and food with oocysts

Drinking water

Recreational water

3. Thick-walled oocyst ingested by host

1. Thick-walled oocyst (sporulated) exits host

© Infobase Publishing

Cryptosporidium passes between hosts in a protective oocyst, which people can pick up by drinking contaminated water.

chemotherapy treatments for cancer, transplant patients, and people infected with HIV, can die from the disease.

Cryptosporidiosis was unknown in humans until 1976 but is now one of the most common waterborne illnesses and is found worldwide. Major outbreaks have even occurred in cities where the municipal water supplies met all federal and state standards. In 1987, in Carrollton, Georgia, 13,000 people were infected with cryptosporidiosis. In 1993, in Milwaukee, Wisconsin, 400,000 people got sick, and some AIDS patients died. More than 1,700 people in Geneva, New York, were sickened by the microbe in 2005 in a play area at a state park where the water had been chlorinated and filtered. In April 2007, the water source for Galway, Ireland, was found to be contaminated, leading to 180 confirmed cases of the disease.

Proper sanitation and sewage treatment have eradicated some waterborne diseases in the developed world, although they are still killers in the developing nations. **Cholera** spreads rapidly through food or drinking water containing infected feces. The pathogen, a comma-shaped bacterium (*Vibrio cholerae*), produces a toxin in its victim's intestines, causing them to expel water and salts from the body. Once the intestines are evacuated, the bacterium multiplies rapidly. Most infected people experience mild or no symptoms, but one in 20 suffers voluminous watery diarrhea, vomiting, and leg cramps. Cholera is easily treated with antibiotics, but if treatment is unavailable, death may occur within hours. At its most virulent, cholera's death rates are as high as 50% for adults and even higher for the elderly, infants, and the otherwise infirm.

Cholera was once much feared throughout the world. The disease was restricted to India until the nineteenth century, when trains and other rapid transportation allowed Europeans to travel between the Indian subcontinent and other parts of the world. Cholera traveled first through the Far East and Russia, moved through Europe, and then reached the Americas. As the epidemic spread across Europe in the early 1830s, lengthy newspaper reports from major European cities reached officials in New York. They used them as a guide and kept their death toll to just over 3,000 by improving sanitation and establishing special cholera hospitals where wastes could be treated safely. It is important to note that these cholera epidemics came decades before the development of the germ theory of disease.

Despite the New World successes, Europeans continued to suffer with cholera. The epidemic of 1848–1849 killed between 50,000 and 70,000 people in England and Wales. In 1854, more than 30,000 people died in London alone. In 1849, John Snow, an English doctor, speculated that the disease was spread through contaminated food and water. Snow had a chance to test his hypothesis during the 1854 epidemic in England. With the epidemic underway, Snow plotted the locations of cholera-related deaths in London. At the time, the city got its water from two water companies, who drew it from the Thames River. One company pumped the water from upstream of London, while the other drew water from downstream. Snow noted that many more people died from using the water that came from downstream (in one neighborhood, 500 people died within 10 days). Snow suggested that these deaths were due to the sewage dumped into the river downstream. To test his hypothesis, the doctor arranged for the pump that supplied the hazardous water to be shut off. Snow's hypothesis paid off: The epidemic was contained. All told, between 1817 and 1917, approximately 38 million people died of cholera in India and about two million in Russia.

Improved sanitation has wiped out cholera in developed nations for more than 100 years. However, cholera still strikes today in developing nations, where many inhabitants do not have access to clean water or cannot access or afford medical treatment. The disease is still common where it began, on the Indian subcontinent, and also in sub-Saharan Africa. The WHO estimates that 120,000 people worldwide die of cholera each year, mostly in Africa. Cholera can reemerge after a long absence. Although South America was free of the disease during most of the twentieth century, an epidemic struck in 1991 and spread into Central America and Mexico, resulting in more than one million cases and more than 10,000 deaths over the next four years.

Pathogens and Water-washed Diseases

Water-washed diseases are diseases that can be stopped or reduced with proper washing. **Trachoma**, the leading cause of preventable blindness in the world, is an example. The bacterium *Chlamydia trachomatis* travels on an infected person's hands or clothing, or on flies that have landed on the discharge emanating from an infected person's eyes or nose. The illness strikes children, damaging the inner eyelid and cornea, but brings on blindness in adults after they have suffered from repeated infections and scarring. Because these victims are usually in their prime years, the disease is an enormous hardship to families and communities. Women are three times more likely to be debilitated by the disease because their care for sick children exposes them to many more infections.

Reference to trachoma appears on papyrus scrolls from ancient Egypt. The disease was a health threat in Europe and the United States into the twentieth century, but it was eradicated by the 1950s

Trachoma is transmitted in unsanitary conditions. It becomes debilitating in women, who are the caregivers of their families. *(Brent Stirton / Getty Images)*

with improved sanitation and living conditions. In impoverished communities in regions of Africa, Asia, the Middle East, and some parts of Latin America and Australia, where access to clean water is limited, nearly everyone suffers from the disease. The WHO estimates that 70 million people are infected with trachoma, and two million people have been blinded by it.

Pathogens and Water-based Diseases

Water-based diseases are caused by aquatic organisms that spend part of their life cycle in the water and another part as parasites. **Schistosomiasis** is caused by five species of parasitic flatworms (blood flukes). Nearly 250 million people in at least 54 countries are infected. Of those, 120 million show symptoms, and 20 million are severely ill. In some parts of the world, particularly in sub-Saharan Africa, where 80% of the cases are found, a large percentage of children under 14 years of age are infected.

Schistosomiasis is common in countries without water treatment facilities. Fishers and farmers contact the parasite in infested surface water in rural areas. The parasite is now spreading into suburban areas as people migrate to the cities. Where schistosomiasis is common, the adults have low work capacity, and the children have slowed growth and poor school performance. Three inexpensive drugs have a 90% success rate in treating the disease. Left untreated, urinary schistosomiasis can lead to bladder cancer: In some areas of Africa, bladder cancer is 32 times more prevalent than it is in the United States.

Pathogens and Water-related Diseases

Water-related diseases are spread by organisms that need water for all or part of their life cycle. Mosquitoes are common disease carriers. Because these insects need water in which to breed, mosquito-borne diseases are prevalent where there is standing water.

The most deadly water-related disease is malaria, which kills more than one million people and causes nearly 400 million cases of acute illness a year. Malaria is most common in sub-Saharan Africa but also occurs in Central and South America, the Mediterranean countries, Asia, and many of the Pacific islands. Many of malaria's victims are under 5 years old; 1 in 20 African children will die of malaria.

Malaria is caused by the protozoan *Plasmodium falciparum,* which is spread to humans by the *Anopheles* mosquito. When an infected mosquito bites, the protozoan passes into the body and enters the red blood cells. The protozoan multiplies and grows in the cells, bursting out every two or three days, which causes the victim to experience a wave of fever. If the disease is not treated, the victim's spleen and liver become enlarged, and blood problems such as anemia (low hemoglobin) and jaundice (high bilirubin) develop. Sufferers may die or may recover temporarily, only to become ill again. When an infected person is bitten by another *Anopheles* mosquito, that mosquito transports the protozoan to new victims.

Malaria was once common in the United States and Europe, but it has been eradicated by the draining of wetlands, better sanitation, and widespread use of the insecticide DDT during the 1950s. Global efforts to eliminate the *Anopheles* mosquito with insecticides during the 1950s and 1960s failed.

Pathogens and Wildlife

Aquatic animals also suffer from pathogens. Pathogenic threats to aquatic ecosystems and global biodiversity are not well understood, but their impact is very likely to be underestimated. Pathogens may be the causes of chronic diseases in wildlife such as ulcers, cancer, and heart disease where infectious agents were not previously suspected. One example of a pathogenic disease in wildlife is botulism, caused by *Clostridium botulinum,* which has brought about substantial waterfowl deaths across Canada.

No group suffers more from pathogens than amphibians, whose populations are plummeting globally. Nearly one third (1,896) of the 5,918 known amphibian species are threatened (compared with 23% of mammals and 12% of birds), and an additional 43% of amphibian species have declining populations. As many as 165 species have become extinct since 1980, according to the Global Amphibian

Frog with a deformed back leg that was collected in Vermont. The deformity was caused by a parasite that has become more prevalent with climate and chemical changes in the regional environment. *(© Michael J. Doolittle / The Image Works)*

Assessment's 2006 report. Many causes have been identified, such as habitat destruction and pollution, and certainly no single cause is to blame. But amphibians are dying off even in ecologically pristine areas, such as national parks in remote areas, where land has been set aside for conservation.

The conclusion researchers have come to is that the primary cause of the decline is a deadly pathogen, *Batrachochytrium dendrobatidis*. This chytrid fungus has reached even the remotest regions. It weakens the animals and destroys their skin: the amphibians are unable to flee from this danger. Nearly 100 species of amphibians in the United States and elsewhere—including Central and South America, Europe, New Zealand, and Australia—have been sickened with the chytrid fungus, and several species are presumed extinct because of it. Colorado boreal toads, which were once common in the lakes, ponds, and streams of the Rocky Mountains, are just one species that is now in sharp decline.

Many researchers think that the pathogens are working in concert with other stresses that threaten amphibians, such as warmer temperatures, increases in ultraviolet radiation (due to depletion of the ozone layer), and pollution. Alternatively, these stresses may make amphibian populations more vulnerable to pathogens. The pathogens spread when infected organisms move from one location to another or when infected alien species are introduced, and the native species are not adapted to fight off the pathogens.

WRAP-UP

Although biological pollutants are living organisms, they are as hazardous to humans and ecosystems as are nonbiological pollutants. The introduction of excess nutrients into aquatic ecosystems brings about eutrophication and dead zones, conditions that completely alter an ecosystem and may bring about the collapse of local fisheries. Introduced species can take over an ecosystem, causing native species to decline or disappear. If the alien organisms are prolific, like zebra mussels, they may infest pipes and other infrastructure, causing millions of dollars in damage each year. Pathogens proliferate where people live in crowded conditions and where water goes untreated. These pathogens cause untold suffering and enormous financial costs due to lost productivity in many countries, particularly those that are already poor.

PART THREE

CLEANING POLLUTED WATERS

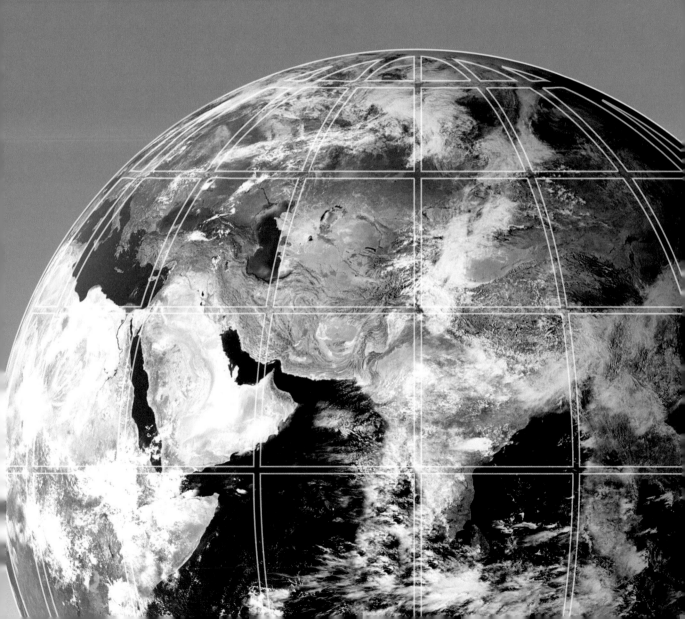

Cleaning Point Source Pollution

For most of human history, wastes were taken care of naturally: Pollutants were diluted, or they dissipated, and they finally disappeared into the waterways. But when human populations grew too large, pollutants built up in the environment, where they festered and caused disease. Point source pollution, primarily coming from sewage, was the first problem to be effectively dealt with. Sewage treatment plants were built before there was any unified response to water pollution. Meanwhile, industrial waste sites were increasing in number and toxicity. The need for a cohesive way of dealing with water pollution led to the passage of the Clean Water Act of 1972. Heavily polluted waste sites are covered under the **Superfund** law of 1980.

THINKING ABOUT POLLUTION PROBLEMS

When determining how to deal with hazardous contaminants, planners try to resolve whether a situation warrants action and, if it does, how much is required. For example, when should a compound no longer be manufactured? How hazardous should a waste disposal site be to warrant being cleaned up? Answering these questions in extreme cases is fairly simple: DDT was destroying the eggs of several species of birds and for that reason was banned for nearly all applications. The Love Canal toxic waste dump, discussed on page 142, was causing disastrous health problems in nearby residents and so had to be cleaned up. But most cases are not so cut and dried, and there is often more than one way to look at many of these situations.

An objective look at a pollution issue often begins with a cost-benefit analysis. In this type of analysis, the monetary benefits of an action are weighed against the monetary value of its costs. The bottom line determines what the response should be. For example, if acid rain can be controlled in part by producing more fuel-efficient cars, the analysis breaks down this way:

⊕ Costs: How much more would a highly fuel-efficient car cost to develop and manufacture? What are the medical costs to those injured if the car is less safe? (Fuel-efficient cars are usually smaller and lighter and more prone to serious damage in accidents.)

⊕ Benefits: How much less is the cost of fuel for a more efficient car? How much money will a recreational fishery in the nearby lakes generate? How much money will be saved by not having to mitigate the damage to the lakes?

It is easy to see from the example above that cost-benefit analyses are not simple and often are inadequate. Some factors are not easily assigned a price. What is the monetary value of swimming in a clean lake or eating a freshly caught, nontoxic fish? How can the cost of potential, rather than actual, pollution problems be assessed? A new chemical with unknown effects may turn out to be completely safe; there will be no cleanup needed, and the cost of cleanup will be nothing. But if the chemical turns out to be harmful, and it is difficult to extract from the environment, the cleanup costs could be enormous.

Another problem with a cost-benefit analysis is that the people paying the costs are often not those getting the benefits. In the acid rain example on page 134, the people who buy the fuel-efficient car will pay the added cost of that car but, in exchange, will get the benefit of lower fuel costs. If that car is less safe, and there is an accident, the car owner's insurance company will pay the medical costs, or—if there is no insurance—either that person or society will bear the costs. In addition, that car owner may never swim in or eat fish from the lake whose health was preserved by the purchase of the fuel-efficient car. On a larger scale, if a company pollutes a region, the company must pay for the cleanup. But because the company is often located far from the site, it will probably see only the costs and not the benefits. The benefits of a cleaner environment are reaped by the local ecosystems and the people who live in that location.

Even if a cost-benefit analysis can be done reasonably, there are still two opposite conclusions that might be drawn from it. For example, in the case of whether a potentially harmful chemical should be manufactured, the two conclusions are these:

- The use of beneficial chemicals, such as pesticides, flame retardants, and gasoline additives should be permitted until scientists are certain that the chemical is harmful.
- Although scientists are not certain that the chemical is harmful, the potential damage outweighs the known benefits, and the manufacture of the chemical should be prohibited until the chemical is proven to be safe.

The second approach is an example of the precautionary principle, an idea that people use every day. Everyone knows to "look before you leap" or that it is "better to be safe than sorry." Another way to state this is that if the consequences of an action are not known, but there is some potential for major or irreversible negative consequences, the action should be avoided.

The precautionary principle places the burden of proof on the groups that advocate the action. By this principle, it is up to the chemical manufacturers to prove that the chemical is not harmful to humans or the environment. This is the opposite of what happens now, when the burden of proof is on environmentalists to prove that the chemical is harmful. This difference is enormously important because the precautionary principle means that only compounds with effects that are understood will be used.

A cost-benefit analysis can also be used to assess whether a site should be cleaned up. Natural processes can handle some pollutants at no cost, but cleaning up many waste sites is an enormous and expensive undertaking.

NATURAL CLEANUP MECHANISMS

As long as the pollutants entering a waterway are not too voluminous or too toxic, natural processes will dilute, disperse, or degrade them. Freshwater added by rain, melting snow and ice, streams, and groundwater dilutes the pollutants. Currents, waves, and seiches disperse the pollutants. Dilution and dispersal working together may reduce the concentrations of pollutants so much that they are not harmful or even detectable. Bacteria may break down contaminants into harmless compounds. Chemical reactions can also break down contaminants, although some breakdown products are as harmful as or even more harmful than the original pollutant.

Wetlands are exceptional pollution cleansers. Contaminants are filtered out of the water by becoming attached to sediment or organic material. Excess nutrients are broken down by bacteria and recycled back into the environment, where they support the ecosystem. Wetlands are so effective at reducing nutrients that researchers estimate that the nitrogen load from the heavily polluted Illinois River basin could be cut in half if 7% of the basin were converted back to wetlands. Increasing rather than decreasing wetlands would be beneficial for future pollution control.

If there are too many pollutants, or if the pollutant levels keep increasing, nature's cleaning mechanisms become overwhelmed. This problem arose in the eighteenth and nineteenth centuries when human populations, agriculture, and industries generated so much pollution that natural water cleansing processes were swamped. Raw sewage, industrial waste, and animal carcasses festered in rivers and lakes, particularly near large industrial cities. Water pollution (coupled with air pollution) made the cities nearly uninhabitable.

London's wake-up call came in 1858, the year of "The Great Stink." With the waste of three million people flowing directly into the Thames and the occurrence of an uncommonly warm summer, the stench from the putrid river brought the city to a standstill. The odor was so bad that sackcloths soaked in chemicals were hung in the windows of the House of Commons so that the legislators could breathe. Perhaps fortunately, this feeble attempt at air purification did not work. Within 18 days, the Members of Parliament resuscitated a bill that had been stalled by government bureaucrats to allow the construction of a massive sewer system, which was constructed to improve the flow of water and traffic along the Thames.

American cities suffered similarly. In 1900, the city of Chicago, Illinois, tried to cut its pollutants by reversing the flow of the Chicago River so that the sewage flowed away from nearby Lake Michigan, into the Illinois River and then downstream to the Mississippi River. While this helped Chicago, it was not a viable solution, as the growing city generated ever more waste while municipalities downstream were swamped with both their own waste and Chicago's. Eventually, a sewage treatment plant was built to treat the waste before the water was returned to the river. The stench and spread of disease made the benefits of these plants far outweigh the costs for these communities.

WASTEWATER TREATMENT

Cleansing water of human waste is the focus of much of the water treatment that takes place in developed nations. The first sewage treatment plant in the United States was built in Washington, D.C., in 1889 to cleanse the foul-smelling, disease-ridden Potomac River. At the time, water quality was the domain of local councils, and there was no coordinated national or international water law.

Wastewater treatment begins right after a toilet is flushed or a bathtub is drained. Pipes run from the house into a sewer main stretching down the street. Water also flows into the sewer main from storm drains. Like small streams coming together to form a large river, small pipes contribute to larger pipes until the sewage reaches the wastewater treatment plant.

Once in the plant, wastewater flows through screens that filter out the large solids. The remainder enters a settling tank, where gravity removes more solids from the mix. The liquid is then filtered through rocks or coke (hard, dry carbon) in basins that are lined with bacteria so that the organic material can be biodegraded. Depending on how clean the treated water must be, the leftover liquid is then passed through even finer sand or earth filters or put through additional biological or chemical cleaning methods. Disease-causing organisms are killed by the addition of chemicals (usually chlorine), by exposure to ultraviolet light, or by microfiltration.

After the water is removed, **sewage sludge** remains. Sewage sludge is transported by pipeline or barges to designated dump sites in inland or oceanic waters. Sludge dumped near the shore becomes diluted as it moves farther out into the water body. However, sewage or ocean sludge sometimes washes onto the shore, with the result that lake beaches are sometimes closed and fishing restricted or banned altogether. Because communities have become increasingly aware of where and how their sewage is dumped, the situation is improving in many locations.

Effective wastewater treatment plants release water that closely matches the stream or lake water the effluent runs into in terms of acidity, nutrients, oxygen, and bacteria. Discharge amounts ranging from 10 million to 100 million gallons per day (38 million to 380 million l) are common for a wastewater treatment plant. In rural areas, where population density is low and wastewater treatment plants are not cost effective, houses have septic systems, which resemble small sewage treatment plants.

THE CLEAN WATER ACT OF 1972

Although the construction of the first wastewater treatment plants was a big step forward, water quality still declined through the twentieth century, particularly during the 1950s and 1960s. Not all cities had sewage treatment plants, and those that did, did not treat all pollutants. The amounts and kinds of chemicals that entered the water escalated. The shift from small farms to more intensive agriculture increased the runoff of nutrients, herbicides, and insecticides. Industrialization and urbanization intensified. Although bits of legislation protecting water and air were enacted as early as 1948, there was no unified national law.

The precipitous decline in water quality came to a head in 1969, when the Cuyahoga River, a tributary of Lake Erie, caught fire as it flowed through downtown Cleveland, Ohio. Although this was not the first time the river had burned, this particular event horrified the nation. The deterioration of the waterways went hand in hand with the corrosion of air quality, as smog alerts plagued many cities, especially Los Angeles and New York City. Rachel Carson's *Silent Spring* in 1962 had made people aware of the deterioration of the natural world; a decade later, they were ready for concrete action.

The early 1970s were a time of great progress for the environment. Two landmark pieces of legislation signed by President Richard Nixon—the Clean Air Act of 1970 and the Clean Water Act of 1972—turned around the deterioration of the air and water of the United States. The Clean Air Act established air quality standards, set emissions limits, empowered state and federal government with enforcement, and increased funding for air pollution research. The law, amended in 1990, now regulates 189 toxic air pollutants, oversees alternative fuels, and also restricts the pollutants that contribute to acid rain and stratospheric ozone depletion. The amended law introduced a market-based system for controlling the emissions that cause acid rain, known as cap-and-trade, which is described in Chapter 11.

The Clean Water Act of 1972 (amended in 1977) protects the surface waters of the United States. The statute uses regulatory and non-regulatory tools to reduce the discharge of pollutants into waterways, to finance wastewater treatment plants, and to manage runoff. The goal is to restore and maintain the cleanliness of the nation's waters for recreation, fishing, and wildlife. The result of the new legislation was the construction of more wastewater treatment plants and controls on the entry of industrial waste into the water supply. Since the passage of the Clean Air Act, point source pollution is tracked down and stopped at its source, when possible.

INDUSTRIAL WASTE SITES

At the same time that sewage treatment was becoming more widespread, industrial wastes were becoming more of a problem. Before state and federal regulations were enacted in the late 1970s, most industrial waste was disposed of in landfills, stored in lagoons or pits, discharged into surface waters with little or no treatment, or burned. Waste mismanagement polluted surface waters, harmed ecosystems, and endangered the health of nearby populations. Three major federal laws—the Resource Conservation and Recovery Act; the Comprehensive Emergency Response, Compensation and Liability Act (CERCLA, also known as Superfund); and the Safe Drinking Water Act—guide the management of hazardous waste. Industrial waste is now disposed of through municipal and industrial wastewater facilities; land disposal facilities, such as landfills, waste pits, and deep underground injection wells; and incineration (which can sometimes produce energy). Some wastes are recycled or converted into nonhazardous material.

Despite these protections, many waste sites still pollute, or threaten to pollute, surface and groundwater. These include old sites that were built before regulations were in place, sites that were improperly built, and those that have experienced more extreme environmental conditions than were planned for (for example, Gulf of Mexico waste sites that were flooded by Hurricane Katrina in 2005).

When action needs to be taken on a waste site, the following steps are involved: First, the site is assessed for contamination. Pollutant levels are analyzed in samples of the soil, surface water, and groundwater. Next, if the site is contaminated, a cost-benefit analysis is performed to determine how much action should be taken. Conclusions are drawn from this analysis. Still, the decision about whether or not to clean up a site depends on the philosophy of the people making the decision. Should they invoke the precautionary principle and perform a cleanup in case the site turns out to be harmful enough to cause serious damage to the environment and people? Or should they wait until the damage has been clearly identified?

Once the analysis has taken place and action has been decided upon, the next step is **remediation**. Remediation removes pollutants from the waterways while also cleaning the land the water comes in contact with, so that the cleaned water is not repolluted. Extremely contaminated sites are placed on the Superfund list, and cleanup is paid for by those who did the damage or with Superfund (CERCLA), a trust fund funded by money collected from the petroleum and chemical industries. At Superfund sites contaminated materials are removed and long-term remedial action plans are implemented. More than 1,200 locations are currently labeled as Superfund sites.

When pollution at a site is not bad enough to warrant a Superfund designation, corporations are asked to take responsibility for cleanup and may be sued if they refuse.

Although many technologies for remediation are now being used, only two of the more innovative approaches will be described here. **Bioremediation** uses the natural biodegrading abilities of microorganisms, such as bacteria, to break down a contaminant. The microorganisms are specially bioengineered to break down a specific contaminant, such as a pesticide. Once an organism is developed, it is bred in large numbers and released into the contaminated water. The

Love Canal and the Origins of Superfund

Like the Cuyahoga River fire, the Love Canal tragedy was a defining moment in the history of water pollution legislation and cleanup in the United States. Love Canal lies less than one mile (1.6 km) from the Niagara River in Niagara Falls, New York. Beginning in the 1940s, the canal was used as a dumpsite by the Hooker Chemical Companies. Approximately 21,000 tons (19,000 metric tons) of chemical wastes were sealed into 55-gallon (200 liter) steel drums and placed in the canal. Engineers thought this disposal method was safe because the canal had been constructed in fairly impermeable ground. In 1953, the company covered the site with dirt and sold it for $1 to the Niagara Falls Board of Education. Although Hooker Chemical warned the Board of Education that the location had been a toxic waste dump, the land became the site of a school, a playground, and 100 homes.

When sewer systems were dug into the impermeable ground, the waste site was breached. As time passed, the steel storage drums rusted, and the chemical wastes leaked out. Toxic pollutants freely traveled through the trenches into nearby areas of the city. Complaints of noxious odors and chemical residue began in the 1960s. When heavy rains created a swamp in 1977, its water contained 82 toxic chemicals, 11 of them suspected human carcinogens. The most prevalent chemical was the carcinogen benzene.

Eckardt C. Beck, an administrator at the Environmental Protection Agency at the time, wrote about the canal area in the *EPA Journal* in 1979:

organism consumes all of the contaminant, and when it has nothing left to eat, it dies out. If practiced correctly, bioremediation should not harm the ecosystem. So far, however, microorganisms that break down all contaminants have not been developed.

In chemical remediation, a chemical compound reacts with a pollutant to produce harmless products. One common substance used for chemical remediation is oxygen, which reacts with the pollutant directly or enhances the ability of biodegrading microorganisms to thrive. Acids or bases also can be used to neutralize contaminants or to cause pollutants to precipitate from the water.

Corroding waste-disposal drums could be seen breaking up through the grounds of backyards. Trees and gardens were turning black and dying. One entire swimming pool had been popped up from its foundation, afloat now on a small sea of chemicals. Puddles of noxious substances were pointed out to me by the residents. Some of these puddles were in their yards, some were in their basements, others yet were on the school grounds. Everywhere the air had a faint, choking smell. Children returned from play with burns on their hands and faces.

People at the school or living nearby developed epilepsy, liver problems, skin sores, rectal bleeding, and severe headaches. Women experienced a high rate of miscarriages, and large numbers of babies were born with birth defects. One girl was born deaf with a cleft palate, an extra row of teeth, and slight retardation.

More than 900 families were evacuated from their homes and relocated in August 1978. This event was a major factor in the passage of the Superfund law in 1980, and Love Canal became a Superfund site in 1983. The land was capped so that rainwater could not reach the waste, a system was built to drain water from the site, debris was cleaned from sewers and creeks, and contaminated soil was removed from residential properties and schools. The containment area is still enforced, but nearby land is now considered environmentally safe and was resettled in the 1990s.

WRAP-UP

For more than a century, sewage treatment plants have made cities inhabitable by cleaning human and animal wastes from the water supply. The Clean Water Act furthered this good work by forcing all municipalities to treat their sewage and to restrict or treat other sources of point source pollution, such as industrial waste. In many ways, the water is much cleaner now than it was in the 1950s and 1960s. But many pollutants are not removed or are only partially removed by wastewater treatment plants, and some pollutants never go through the process. These particular issues are explored in the following chapter.

Modern Water Cleanup Issues

This chapter explores how, since the passage of the Clean Water Act, water pollution problems have grown in areas that the legislation does not adequately cover: non-point source pollution, newly developed toxic chemicals, nutrients, thermal pollution, invasive species, and groundwater pollution. By the late 1980s, point source pollution had been dealt with sufficiently enough that officials were then able to tackle the problem of non-point source pollution. However, this type of pollution is more difficult to control because a single responsible party often cannot be identified. At the same time, acid rain was being recognized as an important problem, and a solution was implemented to restrict atmospheric acid production.

REDUCING ACID RAIN

As is true with other types of pollution control, limiting the creation of acid rain is far easier than dealing with acid damage in the environment. Reducing acid rain requires reducing emissions of the gases that cause it: SO_2 and NO_x. Great progress has been made by using a unique, market-based approach to reduce SO_2—and, more recently, NO_x—as outlined in the 1990 Amendment to the Clean Air Act.

Improvements in SO_2 and NO_x pollution are attributed primarily to controls implemented under the Environmental Protection Agency's (EPA) Acid Rain Program, which began in 1995. This cap-and-trade program requires the EPA to set a countrywide cap for annual SO_2 emissions. The total amount of allowed emissions is divided among program participants who receive allowances for the amount of SO_2 they are permitted to discharge each year. The allowances can be used, traded to another participant, or banked for future use. Because allowances can be traded for cash, companies have a monetary incentive to develop emission-saving technologies. If a participant exceeds its total allowances—those that it has been assigned this year and those it has banked for future use—it is fined. To be sure that emissions lessen over time, the EPA has set a cap that decreases each year until the permanent cap is reached in 2010. At that time, annual SO_2 emissions will be approximately 50% below 1980 levels. The success of cap-and-trade for SO_2 has resulted in a new program being set up to regulate NO_x. This was not done initially because NO_x comes from a much wider variety of sources and is therefore harder to control. Nonetheless, a limited program has been initiated to regulate NO_x emissions coming from power plants and from motor vehicles in some eastern and midwestern states.

Environmentalists and business people have strongly supported cap-and-trade programs for the reduction of acid rain–causing pollutants, and the programs have been very successful. With a compliance level of over 99%, pollutant emissions have been greatly reduced. By 2005, SO_2 emissions were 41% lower than in 1980 and NO_x emissions were less than half what they would likely have been without the program. This has resulted in a decrease in acid deposition of as much as 36% in the acid-prone regions of the eastern United States, when compared with 1980 levels. In some areas, the number of acidic lakes and streams has decreased by one-quarter to one-third, although in some areas there has been no change. Since the early 1990s, the number of acidic lakes in the Adirondacks has decreased from 13% to 8% of what they were.

Cap-and-trade systems have been proposed for wider adoption but are difficult to implement because the number of pollutants and their behavior after their emission is complex. Mercury, for example, has been the subject of recent disagreements. A cap-and-trade program for mercury would allow a single polluter, or polluters from a single geographical area, to buy or trade for pollution credits, possibly resulting in high concentrations of the metal in some locations. Because airborne mercury travels far from its source, atmospheric processes might also concentrate the fallout. Either of these scenarios could create mercury "hot spots" in which concentrations of the metal were far higher than is safe. Because mercury is extremely toxic, especially to children and fetuses, locally high levels of the compound could cause acute damage to nearby residents. Cap-and-trade programs work for other pollutants because the effects of a locally high concentration of the compound are not so dire.

The alternative (and far inferior) approach to reducing the acidity of rainfall is to mitigate the damage caused by acid rain. Just as rocks containing calcium carbonate buffer acidic water in nature, lime that has been added to lakes or ponds can also buffer acidic water. The downside to this is that while the carbonate neutralizes the water, it does nothing to change soil chemistry or improve forest health. This approach is also expensive and must be done repeatedly for the benefit to be felt. Despite these drawbacks, countries such as Sweden and Norway, which have little control over the acid rain they receive, treat lakes and ponds this way with the hopes that native fish populations will survive until the situation improves. In the eastern United States, adding lime to the soil has improved the health and productivity of maple trees used by the maple syrup industry. In this particular case, the expense is worth the economic value of maple syrup.

NUTRIENTS

Nutrient pollution is thought to be the most serious problem facing many waterways in the United States. Many scientists think that current voluntary measures are not sufficient to reduce nutrient pollution significantly in areas such as the Gulf of Mexico dead zone. Suggestions for a remedy include a designated federal cap on nitrate emissions for each state, with a provision that would give states the flexibility to target the regions where a reduction in nitrate pollution would have the greatest impact.

A cap-and-trade program has been proposed for nutrients. Under this program, the federal government would evaluate watersheds to determine the amount of nutrients that could be released within them during one year. Program participants would receive a portion of this amount as their nutrient discharge allowance, which could be used, traded to another participant, or banked for future use. Participants would be fined if they exceeded their allowance. Cap-and-trade programs for nutrients are being tried in the Kalamazoo River basin and on the Potomac River and the Chesapeake Bay system.

Family-operated farms can reduce nutrient pollution by reducing the runoff from their fields. Controlling drainage keeps more water in the ground, rather than allowing it to escape into waterways. Planting crops that cover the ground year round rather than only part of the year and constructing well-placed wetlands around the fields are both methods that help reduce runoff. Once excess nutrients are in the water, sewage treatment plants can be outfitted to remove them more effectively.

Factory farms contribute nutrients, pharmaceuticals, pathogens, and other pollutants to the water supply. While the best approach for reducing pollution from these mega-farms would be to encourage a return to smaller, family-operated farms, this is unlikely to happen on a large scale very quickly. Some recommendations for cleaning up factory farm wastes include banning new open-air manure lagoons, ceasing aerial spraying of liquid wastes, and phasing out existing lagoon/sprayfield operations. Another recommendation for managing these farms is to require them to participate fully in the provisions of the Clean Water Act.

In some locations, wetlands are being constructed to treat nutrients and other runoff from farms, parking lots, and small wastewater treatment plants. New York City is spending $1 billion to conserve and protect the source of the city's drinking water in upstate New York. The alternative would be to spend $5 billion on a state-of-the-art water filtration plant that would cost an additional $300 million a year to operate.

TOXIC CHEMICALS

While nutrients are recognized as an enormous water pollution problem, toxic chemicals have not received much attention. Although groups of researchers are working to understand health effects like endocrine disruption, these problems are just beginning to receive widespread notice. While several toxic chemicals have been banned—DDT, chlordane, toxaphene, and PCBs, among others—many related chemicals remain on the market and new ones are being introduced each year. Because the burden of proof is on scientists to show that a chemical being used is harmful before it is restricted, little can be done to keep a new chemical from entering the market.

Environmental groups advocate the use of the precautionary principle to guide the manufacture and use of potentially toxic chemicals. Modern chemicals are well fit for applying this principle: The health and environmental effects of these chemicals can be dire; there is little information on most of them; doing well-run scientific experiments can take years; the actions of these chemicals in the environment are unpredictable and complex; and once the chemicals are spread into the environment, they are very difficult to remove. These groups recommend that chemicals not be used until their effects on human health and the environment are known. However, chemical manufacturers and people who rely on the benefits these chemicals provide do not agree. If there is an issue with a chemical, the outcome is determined by politicians or in the courts. Politicians, lawyers, and jurors, however, are rarely trained to evaluate and weigh scientific information.

Many toxic and potentially toxic chemicals enter the environment all the time, so the next step is to deal with them once they are there.

Many communities are looking at wastewater treatment systems that can handle some of these toxic chemicals.

REDUCING THERMAL POLLUTION

Thermal pollution is a large, barely discussed problem that is solvable. Returning cooling water to its source at roughly the same temperature it was before its removal requires cooling methods that are available. But these methods are more expensive than those currently used by power plants and industrial plants. Some solutions to the thermal pollution problem are

- using and wasting less electricity
- limiting the amount of heated water discharged into the same body of water
- diluting the warm water with cooler water before releasing it into the environment
- returning the warm water to locations that are less ecologically vulnerable
- using cooling towers to transfer heat to the atmosphere
- allowing water to cool in shallow ponds or canals and reusing it.

Plant operators are considering alternative water supplies to cool power and industrial plants. **Degraded water** is surface water, groundwater, treated municipal effluent, or industrial wastewater that is too contaminated for drinking but could be used for cooling. **Reclaimed water** is wastewater that has been used in another industrial process. Using alternative water supplies such as these for cooling would free up freshwater sources for municipal and agricultural uses.

Engineers may someday design a system that could convert a portion of the wasted heat into electricity, which would increase the electrical output of power plants without generating additional pollution. So far, the technology is extremely inefficient and can convert only

17% of the heat into electricity. For such a system to be cost effective, it should be at least 25% efficient.

SEDIMENT

Stopping sediment pollution is difficult because the sediment sources are scattered around the watershed. No-till farming and constructing stream bank fencing are two ways that farmers can prevent soil erosion. Taking individual trees rather than clear-cutting is one way the logging industry could minimize soil erosion.

GROUNDWATER CLEANUP

It has already been mentioned that keeping contaminants out of the water is easier and cheaper than cleaning the water once it has been contaminated. If this is true of surface water, then it is exponentially true of groundwater. The primary reason for this is that groundwater is so difficult to access.

The natural cleansing that takes place in surface waters happens to a much lesser extent in groundwater. These waters move slowly, and pollutants are not flushed out as they are in streams and lakes. The oxygen that bacteria need for biodegrading is in short supply in groundwater.

Contaminated water in an aquifer is difficult to get to and in some cases must be removed from the aquifer for cleaning. Because decontaminating the water does no good if the rock and soil it travels through are contaminated, these materials must be cleaned as well. Thoroughly cleaning an aquifer requires cleansing each pore within the soil or rock unit. For this reason, cleaning polluted groundwater is very costly, takes years, and is sometimes not technically feasible. If the toxic materials can be removed from the aquifer, safely disposing them is another challenge.

There are four stages in cleansing a contaminated groundwater aquifer. First, hydrologists eliminate the source of the pollution. If the source is an underground tank, the tank must be pumped dry and then dug out from the ground. If the source is a factory that is releasing toxic chemicals, the factory may be required to stop the discharge. If the source is a toxic waste dump, the site must be decontaminated.

Second, the hydrologists monitor the extent and concentration of the contamination. They must sample the water to determine how far, in what direction, and how rapidly the plume of polluted water is moving. They must determine the concentration of the contaminant to calculate how much it is being diluted. For water sampling, the scientists use existing wells where possible and drill test wells where necessary to check for pollutant concentrations.

Third, hydrologists develop computer models using information on the permeability of the aquifer and the direction and rate of groundwater flow, among other features, to locate the plume and predict the direction of the contaminant dispersal through the aquifer.

The final stage is for remediation of the aquifer, which has several steps. First an underground barrier is constructed to isolate the contaminated groundwater from the rest of the aquifer. Next, the contaminated water must be treated. If possible, it is treated in place by bioremediation, which has many advantages over other cleanup methods. Microorganisms can be injected into the aquifer via wells. They can then travel through the pores of the aquifer unassisted. Air may be pumped into the polluted region to encourage the growth and reproduction of the microbes. Bioremediation can be easily monitored by watching the chemical reactions that are taking place in the fluid or rock material. Because it does not involve excavation of large amounts of material, bioremediation within the aquifer is relatively inexpensive.

If bioremediation is not feasible, other techniques can be used. With chemical remediation, the chemical is pumped into the aquifer so that the contaminant is destroyed. Acids or bases can neutralize contaminants or cause pollutants to precipitate from the water. Other more invasive techniques include air stripping, advanced oxidation, granular activated carbon (GAC), and soil vapor extraction (SVE), which are described on page 153. The most difficult option is for reclamation teams to pump the water to the surface, cleanse it using chemical or biological remediation, and then reinject it into the aquifer. In this case, the contaminated portions of the aquifer must be dug up and the pollutant destroyed by incinerating or chemically processing the soil, which is then returned to the ground. This technique is often prohibitively expensive and is done only in extreme cases.

The case of methyl tertiary-butyl ether (MTBE) provides an example of how groundwater becomes polluted and what is necessary to clean it. MTBE was used as a gasoline additive between 1992 and 1998, until the EPA classified it as a potential human carcinogen. Ready-to-pump gasoline, including its additives, is stored in underground tanks at service stations. According to a report from the Association of Metropolitan Water Agencies issued in June 2005, tens of thousands of these tanks have leaked, leading to MTBE contamination in approximately 300 water systems in 36 states. MTBE-contaminated water smells like turpentine. The chemical is especially toxic when breathed; because it vaporizes in hot water, showering in the contaminated water is more dangerous than drinking it.

Since 2003, bioremediation has been under way on a massive MTBE plume in the San Fernando Valley of California. The San Fernando Valley groundwater supplies 10% of the city's drinking water. The source of the plume is a gas station in North Hollywood, which has since been shut down. A thick layer of gasoline originating from this station now floats on the area's groundwater. Analyses of the water show concentrations of up to 100,000 ppb MTBE—safe levels for drinking are 5 ppb. When the plume was found to be migrating toward Los Angeles, two groundwater pumps were shut down so that the contamination would not be sucked closer to the city.

MTBE was thought to be resistant to biodegradation until Professor Kate Scow of the University of California, Davis, discovered MTBE-loving microbes, called PM1, in groundwater. PM1 like to ingest carbon, and when they are cultivated inside carbon filters, their numbers soar. Contaminated water is pumped into a system containing these bacteria for bioremediation. After several trips, the

MTBE levels drop below 0.5 ppb (the detection limit) and the clean water is reinjected back into the aquifer. Reinjection saves 10 million gallons (38 billion l) of water a year that might otherwise be lost from the drinking water supplies.

Other methods of decontaminating MTBE in aquifers are more difficult and expensive. In air stripping, contaminated water is pumped through packing material that is exposed to air, which removes the chemicals. The advanced oxidation method uses ultraviolet light and chemicals for chemical remediation. In granular activated carbon (GAC) treatment, the polluted water is pumped through activated carbon to remove the organic material. This technique works well with gasoline compounds such as benzene, but because MTBE does not readily stick to carbon, the water must be pumped through the carbon many times. In soil vapor extraction (SVE), air pumped through the soil vaporizes the MTBE, which is then extracted from the soil and treated.

Depending on the method used and the extent of the contamination, a nationwide cleanup of MTBE is estimated to cost between $20 billion and $100 billion. Oil companies say they should have only limited financial liability because the government required the inclusion of oxygenate additives in gasoline. But, as Paul J. Granger, the superintendent of the Plainview, Long Island, water system, told *The New York Times* in 2004, "There are reams of documents indicating that oil companies knew the dangers of MTBE, but these companies opted to use MTBE because it was the cheapest [gasoline additive]." Groundwater in Granger's district is polluted with 2,000 times the allowable MTBE level, and the cleanup is estimated to cost between $390 million to $1 billion, an amount the small community simply cannot afford.

New York and many other states have banned MTBE, but the damage has already been done. "People seem to be waiting for some major disaster," Walter L.T. Hang, president of Toxics Targeting (a provider of environmental data to environmental consultants and drinking water suppliers), said to *The New York Times* in 2004. "But the disaster is already here. It just happens to be occurring underground."

WATER POLLUTION IN DEVELOPING NATIONS

In the developing nations, the population is growing rapidly; in many of them, development is expanding swiftly, as well. With the limited funds available going into much needed economic development, governments have little money left to allot for water quality protection. On average, 90% to 95% of domestic sewage and 75% of industrial waste go into surface waters without any treatment. In these countries, human and animal waste is still the largest problem.

Economic development can be hard on a nation's waterways. Although the economies of China and India are booming, many of China's major rivers are so polluted with toxins and sediments that the fisheries have collapsed. All of India's 14 major rivers are badly polluted. Many rivers in Thailand and Malaysia contain 30 to 100 times more pathogens, heavy metals, and toxic chemicals than is permitted by government health standards.

REDUCING AN INDIVIDUAL'S CONTRIBUTIONS TO WATER POLLUTION

The best way for anyone to reduce his or her contribution to pollution is to consume less: less energy, less water, fewer material goods. Pollutants are the byproduct of the lifestyle people in the developed world take for granted. Pollutants are generated when we power up our computers, cook our meals, or drive to a baseball game. They are also created during the manufacture of products, such as personal stereos and cars. Everyone's house, lawn, and pets contribute to water pollution, as do nearby roadways. Reducing the pollutants we manufacture is as easy as reducing the amount of energy we use, the number of products we consume, and the amount of fertilizers and pesticides we use in our gardens. While these strategies require some thought—and perhaps sacrifice—they can yield important returns.

Reducing energy consumption contributes enormously to reducing water pollution. It decreases nitrate pollution and acid rain by reducing air pollution. The major source of air pollution created by people in the developed world involves transportation. For ideas on how to reduce pollution from transportation sources, see the table below.

The table on page 156 gives ideas for how to reduce energy consumption at home.

There are also ways to minimize an individual's contribution to water pollution, particularly regarding runoff.

⊕ Conserve water: Use efficient plumbing fixtures, take shorter showers, place toilet dams or bricks in toilet tanks, use low-flow toilets and showerheads, repair drips, sweep driveways instead of hosing them down, and direct roof runoff onto vegetation for use by plants. Wash the car with a bucket of

Reducing Pollution from Transportation

WHAT TO DO	HOW TO DO IT
Use less gasoline	Use public transportation, walk, ride a bike, carpool.
Buy a "green" vehicle	Choose an EPA-approved vehicle (see link in "Further Reading and Web Sites") that emits less pollution, including greenhouse gases.
Look into new technologies	Check out hybrid cars, or cars powered by liquid natural gas or fuel cells, to see whether they are cost effective.
Be frugal when driving	Avoid drive-through lines; keep car serviced and tires inflated; stay within the speed limit; do not accelerate quickly.
Be careful when filling the gas tank	Fill during the cooler evening hours to avoid evaporation; as the saying goes, "don't spill or overfill."

Reducing Energy Consumption in the Home

WHAT TO DO	HOW TO DO IT
Use energy-efficient appliances	Purchase energy-efficient appliances and lighting; be sure they are operating well; be sure woodstoves and fireplaces are well maintained.
Save electricity	Turn off the lights, television, and computer, especially overnight; keep the thermostat set to reasonable temperatures.
Use vegetation	Plant deciduous trees around the house to provide shade in the summer and to let in warmth and light during the winter.
Consume sensibly	Buy only products that are really needed; buy products that are energy efficient.
Reduce, reuse, and recycle	Recycling materials uses less energy than making a new product from new materials. Choose recycled products and those that have less packaging. Reusing products is even better.

soapy water and turn off the hose when it is not being used, or use a car wash that recycles water.

⊕ Dispose of hazardous household products correctly, using methods recommended by the local sanitation department. Do not put paints, used oil, solvents, polishes, pool chemicals, insecticides, or other harmful chemicals into drains or toilets. Dispose of motor oil properly, not in storm drains.

⊕ Recycle used motor oil and do not dump it into sewers or onto the ground. One quart (1 liter) of motor oil can pollute up to 250,000 gallons (946 cubic m) of groundwater.

⊕ Whenever possible, use environmentally sensitive products such as organic pesticides. See the EPA's EnviroSense Web site, listed in the Further Reading and Web Sites section for suggested substitutes for toxic products.

⊕ Dispose of trash properly; recycle when possible. Clean up after pets.

⊕ Reduce the use of artificial fertilizers, or use natural fertilizers: compost, manure, bone meal, or peat.

⊕ Do not overwater lawns and gardens. Use the drip method to water the plants that need it. Reducing the amount of water running through the soil decreases the amount of fertilizer that is leached from it.

⊕ Increase surfaces that allow drainage, such as vegetation, gravel, and wood decking, while decreasing impervious surfaces, such as concrete, bricks, and flat stones. Direct rain gutters and downspouts to areas that will drain, rather than to impervious areas.

WRAP-UP

Cleaning up some water pollutants is not as simple as sending water through a wastewater treatment plant. Much of the water that runs off urbanized or agricultural regions does not run through plants, and many of the chemicals found in that water are not filtered by treatment systems. Reducing the amount of certain types of pollutants that enter the environment has been very effective in reducing some types of pollution, as has been done in cap-and-trade systems for acid rain-causing pollutants. Cap-and-trade systems are now being recommended for nutrients in waterways where eutrophication is a problem. Groundwater pollution is very difficult and expensive to mitigate because the contamination plume is difficult to get to and difficult to clean. The best way to keep the waterways clean is to reduce the amount of pollution that gets into them. This requires people to consume less and to be careful how they use water and the substances that may contaminate it.

The History of
Water Pollution in
the Great Lakes

The history of water pollution in the Great Lakes parallels the history of water pollution in the developed countries. For decades, people believed that the enormous amount of water in the lakes would dilute any substance that was put into them. But only one percent of the water that enters the lakes each year flows out, so most pollutants that enter the lakes accumulate. At first, sewage brought stench and disease. Later on, industrial wastes grew in volume to become a problem. By the 1950s and 1960s, the lakes were barely alive. Measures taken after the passage of the Clean Water Act greatly improved the situation. But the lakes are still polluted—indeed, they are at a crisis point now—primarily from toxic chemicals and invasive species.

EARLY GREAT LAKES POLLUTION

As Europeans settled the Great Lakes drainage basin, the forests were logged to obtain lumber and to create farmland, while the water was polluted with sediment that buried ecosystems and clogged the breathing mechanisms of aquatic animals. As municipalities and industries grew up in the lake basin, they ran sewage and industrial waste pipes directly into the lakes and their tributary streams. Chemical fertilizers and phosphorus-rich detergents drowned the lakes in excess nutrients, resulting in eutrophication and extensive fish kills. Pesticides such as DDT damaged wildlife populations, particularly bald eagles, hawks, and mink. Pulp and papers mills added sawdust and chemical pollution, including extremely toxic mercury. Worst off was the shallowest lake, Lake Erie, which was declared "dead" from nutrient overload and toxic chemicals in the 1960s. The lake's putrid surface was covered with decaying plant matter, detergent suds, and lifeless fish.

No one said much about the pollution until the Cuyahoga River in Ohio caught fire in 1969. The visual impact of a burning river in a major American city served as the turning point for national awareness of the immense problem of water pollution.

Even children were made aware of the issue. In 1971, Dr. Seuss (Theodor Seuss Geisel) immortalized Lake Erie's problems in his book *The Lorax*. Controversial at the time, the book's environmentalist character, the Lorax (who speaks for the trees) tells the "Once-ler" (who is turning "truffula trees" into useless "thneeds" and polluting the air and water as he does):

> You're glumping the pond where the Humming-Fish hummed!
> No more can they hum, for their gills are all gummed.
> So I'm sending them off. Oh, their future is dreary.
> They'll walk on their fins and get woefully weary
> in search of some water that isn't so smeary.
> I hear things are just as bad up in Lake Erie.

The Cuyahoga fire led Canada and the United States to sign the Great Lakes Water Quality Agreement in 1972, the same year the United States passed the Clean Water Act. The nations agreed to regulate phosphorus runoff and to encourage water quality research and

Industrial pollution in Indiana Harbor on the southwestern shore of Lake Michigan, near Chicago, in 1968. *(United States Environmental Protection Agency, Region V)*

monitoring. In just a few years, only half as much phosphate was entering Lake Erie daily, and the lake's color turned from green to blue. An amended and more far-reaching agreement on the lakes was signed by Canada and the United States in 1978. It aimed to restore and maintain the chemical, physical, and biological integrity of the Great Lakes ecosystem by reducing phosphorus and eliminating the further introduction of POPs into the lakes. The most recent amendment, in 1987, regulates non-point source pollution, contaminated sediments, and airborne pollutants. This amendment helps to identify areas of concern to be addressed and management plans to be drawn.

The combined federal and state regulations dramatically altered the quality of water entering the Great Lakes. Since the early 1970s, nearly all industrial plants that were polluting the lakes and streams in the drainage basin have been outfitted with control devices to reduce their toxic discharge. The number of sewage treatment facilities has doubled. Phosphate detergents and other cleaners rich in nutrients have been eliminated.

CURRENT PROBLEMS IN GREAT LAKES POLLUTION

These changes tremendously improved water quality in all of the Great Lakes and many tributaries. By 1991, Lake Erie was so much cleaner that Dr. Seuss removed the Lake Erie line from *The Lorax*; it does not appear in current editions. But though Lake Erie's fish no longer choke on "gluppity-glup," the situation in the Great Lakes is still grim. Development along the shores has damaged wetlands and offshore lake habitat so that native species continue to suffer. Pollutants that were added to the lakes, before the cleanup that began in the 1970s remain in the lakes and new chemicals are being added. PCBs, mercury, and other chemicals that adhered to lake sediments and settled to the bottom are continually being dredged up in efforts to keep shipping channels open. Carcinogenic asbestos released by the steel industry has buried the floor of the western segment of Lake Superior. Agricultural runoff, detergents, and incompletely treated sewage continue to enter Lake Erie, still the most polluted of the lakes.

Perhaps the largest problem for the Great Lakes now is contamination by nonnative species of plants and animals, which is irrevocably altering the ecology of the entire Great Lakes ecosystem. The sea lamprey decimated native fish populations between the 1920s and mid-1950s, when a poison that kills sea lamprey larvae was discovered. More recently, the chemicals that lampreys use to attract mates have been used to round up the adults and remove them from the ecosystem.

The 1959 opening of the St. Lawrence Seaway, which connects the lakes with the Atlantic Ocean, brought an explosion in the number of nonnative species in the lakes as more and more ships have dumped ballast water drawn from around the world into the ecosystem. Today, at least 180 nonnative species lurk in the lakes; and a new one arrives, on average, every eight months. Some invasions have been contained,

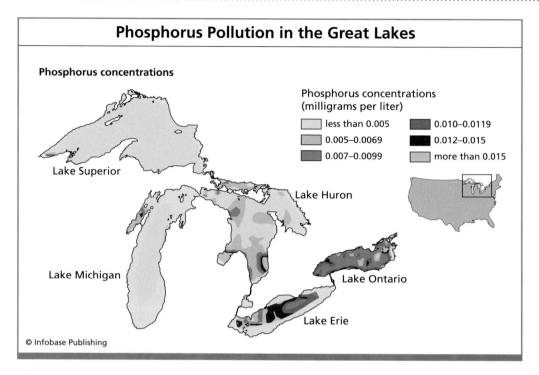

Phosphorus Pollution in the Great Lakes

Phosphorus concentrations

Phosphorus concentrations
(milligrams per liter)

less than 0.005   0.010–0.0119
0.005–0.0069   0.012–0.015
0.007–0.0099   more than 0.015

Lake Superior

Lake Huron

Lake Michigan

Lake Ontario

Lake Erie

© Infobase Publishing

This map shows phosphorus concentrations in the Great Lakes arising from pollution by detergents, sewage treatment, and fertilizer runoff.

such as that of the alewife (*Alosa pseudoharengus*), a beach-fouling fish that was controlled by planting hundreds of millions of Pacific salmon to eat the invaders.

By far the most destructive invader to date has been the zebra mussel. These tiny mollusks were first discovered in the summer of 1988 in Lake St. Clair by a student on a field trip. A sample had to be sent to Europe for identification. Initially, zebra mussels seemed harmless. They had even been planted by the Dutch to clean up some of their more polluted waters. But with no native predator in the Great Lakes, the population growth of the tiny mussels is now out of control. Zebra mussels (along with quagga mussels) have now spread to all the Great Lakes and are showing up in inland waterways and lakes throughout North America. The mussels' tiny larvae are spread by lake currents, by boats traveling between the lakes, by fishing gear, and by anything else they can latch on to.

Zebra mussels filter enormous quantities of water. In 1991, Professor Hugh MacIsaac of the University of Windsor created a computer model that included the number of zebra mussels that were likely on the bottom of Lake Erie and the amount of water a single mussel could filter. "I couldn't believe it," he told the *Milwaukee Journal Sentinel* in 2004. "It was telling me that these mussels were conceivably filtering western Lake Erie seven times per day—filtering all of the water to strip the food seven times in one day."

Filtering has improved the lakes' water clarity but has also altered the lakes' ecology. While zebra mussels consume nearly everything in the water, they let microscopic blue-green algae pass through their

Zebra mussels washed up on a beach on Lake Erie. *(Great Lakes Environmental Research Lab / NOAA)*

filtration systems unharmed. These microcystis algae now thrive in the lakes, but they are toxic and can poison pets, livestock, and even humans. At this time, Michigan's Muskegon Lake has microcystin levels 10 times higher than what the World Health Organization (WHO) considers safe for swimming. Microcystis algae populations are high when the lakes are full of excess nutrients, but their populations decline along with nutrient levels.

Other algae have been thriving as a result of the zebra mussel invasion. Clearer water has allowed photosynthesizing algae to grow on the bottoms of the shallow portions of the lakes, which has led to eutrophication. Some beaches along Lake Michigan stink of rotting sewage, but the actual cause is rotting cladophora, a bright green algae that grows on the bottom of the lake like a thick lawn. When the algae die, as they inevitably do, an algae mass washes ashore and decomposes, causing the noxious smell.

"It's unbearable, and you say to yourself: What is going on?" said Sheldon Wasserman, physician and state representative, in the *Milwaukee Journal Sentinel* in 2004. "We have this beautiful natural wonder, one of the greatest freshwater lakes in the world, and . . . it basically looks like a disaster."

Animals higher in the ecosystem are affected by the zebra mussels as well. In Lake Erie, lake-bottom algae are decomposed by anaerobic bacteria that cause botulism. Zebra mussels filter water and eject the bacteria, which are then eaten by the goby (*Neogobius melanostomus*), an alien fish species from Europe. Botulism paralyzes the gobies, making them easy prey for birds such as loons, grebes, and gulls, which are then afflicted with botulism. Tens of thousands of birds have died in Lake Erie alone.

Zebra mussels are not the only invasive mussel species. Quagga mussels (*Dreissena rostriformis bugensis*), an alien species from the Caspian Sea that arrived in the Great Lakes in 1991, are bringing about the collapse of the bottom of the Great Lakes food web. Before quagga mussels, the tiny, shrimplike diporeia, only one-quarter inch (64 cm) long, blanketed the bottom of Lake Michigan. This crustacean served as a major food source for native whitefish—a prized game fish—and as a part of the diet of small game fish such as chubs, alewives, and smelt, which in turn are preyed upon by salmon and trout. Scientists once found up to 20,000 diporeia per square meter; now there are vast areas where few or none are found. No one knows exactly how the mussels are killing off the diporeia; they may simply be filtering all the diporeia's food. Without their favorite food, Lake Ontario's whitefish are starving. Whitefish sometimes try to eat zebra mussels, but because they do not have teeth, they are unable to crack the zebra mussel's shell to get to the meat.

These ecological changes have enormous consequences for the recreational fishing industry of the Great Lakes. Wisconsin's Lake Michigan perch population has declined by about 90% in the last decade, and commercial harvests were stopped on Lake Michigan in 1996, except in the waters of Green Bay. Milwaukee's famous Friday night fish fries now usually serve fish caught in Canada or Europe. Perch may be suffering due to overfishing, collapse of the food web due to the zebra mussels, or improved water clarity leading to more predation. Competition with the perchlike ruffe (*Gymnocephalus cernuus*) and the goby, both alien species, has further decreased perch populations.

The future does not look bright for native species. Two types of invasive crustaceans are now becoming established in the lakes' food web. The spikes on these crustaceans' backs make them inedible to the lakes' native fish. Scientists predict that it is only a matter of time for two new species of shrimp to arrive: one that kills organisms, sometimes without eating them, and another that coats the bottom of a lake with tubes of mud. The Asian carp, an escapee from fish farms, is moving up the Mississippi and Illinois rivers toward Lake Michigan. Thus far, it has been kept away by a temporary electric barrier.

Zebra and quagga mussels take a tremendous economic toll on human development. Billions of zebra mussels plug pipes at power plants and city drinking systems each year, with costs of $100 million to the power industry and other users. In all, the General Accounting Office of the United States estimates that zebra mussels cost $300 million per year.

THE PRESENT AND FUTURE OF THE GREAT LAKES

Until recently, a number of federal and state agencies from the United States and Canada have been overseeing the problems of the Great Lakes. Lack of coordination has been cited as one problem in trying to make planning, monitoring, cleanup, and restoration efforts work. In 2005, a coalition of government agencies including the Environmental Protection Agency (EPA), businesses, and environmental groups such as the National Wildlife Federation released a blueprint for fixing the Great Lakes. The total cost could be up to $20 billion in federal, state, and private money.

The plan includes:

- upgrading antiquated municipal sewer systems
- reducing agricultural runoff
- restoring 550,000 acres (222,577 hectares) of wetlands (about 50% of wetlands around the lakes have already been lost)
- controlling the spread of alien species by constructing barriers and monitoring equipment and initiating other controls
- cleaning polluted harbors and bays.

As Tom Kiernan, president of the National Parks Conservation Association, said to *The New York Times* in 2005, "The Great Lakes are seriously ill. This draft plan is a very good first step in restoring the Great Lakes to health."

Conclusion

Water is one of the most precious commodities that Earth provides. This unique substance is indispensable to all living creatures. Water helps human society to thrive: It is necessary for growing food, generating power, and manufacturing modern consumer goods. Waterways have long been used to transport goods and people into and out from continental interiors. They were essential in the past for establishing towns, cities, and even empires. The Roman Empire would not have been seated in central Italy had it not been for the Tiber River. New York City would not be the economic capital of the New World if it were not at the confluence of the Hudson River and the Atlantic Ocean.

People engineer waterways to make them more useful. Dams assure that a region has a year-round supply of water and can also provide hydroelectric power, which is inexpensive and clean. Dams, levees, and other structures protect riverbank development from floods. But waterway engineering comes at a cost: Without annual floods, nutrients are no longer spread onto floodplains; dams may cause regions of social, cultural, and recreational value to be submerged beneath the water; and providing protection from flooding may cause more development along a river, so that if a catastrophic flood occurs, the damage is greater than it might have been otherwise.

Habitat destruction, from ruinous fishing techniques, bad aquaculture practices, or coastal development, destroys the ecosystems in which aquatic organisms live and drives their populations down. Habitat destruction also impairs the services that these ecosystems provide, such as pollutant filtering by wetlands. To protect important habitats, development must be discouraged in sensitive regions, susceptible habitats must be protected, and damaged habitats must be restored where possible. It is important to keep in mind that it is easier to protect a natural habitat such as a wetland than to try to build a replacement. Conservation of valuable habitats is the better choice.

Inland waters have long been used as a dumping ground for pollutants. This practice has only magnified as populations have grown and industrialization and intensive agriculture have become more widespread. The dumping of raw sewage was the problem for many decades, but the use of sewage treatment plants has reduced that source of pollution greatly, at least in the developed countries. Since the early 1970s, when legislation designed to protect water and air was implemented, water pollution sources have been regulated and monitored and mechanisms have been put in place for implementing cleanup. As a result, rivers in the United States no longer catch fire, acid rain that spreads pollutants is in decline, and eutrophication is being reduced. Despite the progress that has been made in the developed countries, however, developing nations continue to be plagued by inadequate sewage disposal and pathogenic disease.

Developed nations still have numerous problems with pollution that, in some ways, are worse than the old problems. Nutrient runoff is so pervasive that it continues to have enormous environmental effects, causing fish kills and creating dead zones, such as the dead zone area in the Gulf of Mexico outward from the Mississippi River delta. Many scientists think that the voluntary nutrient-reduction programs now in place are not enough to halt a worsening of these conditions, and that programs such as a cap-and-trade program for managing nutrients within a watershed should be implemented. Indeed, some researchers think that the Gulf of Mexico ecosystem is in danger of collapsing, something that has already happened to the Black Sea. But ecosystems are so complex that it is difficult to know if, when, or how this will occur.

Invasive species are an exploding problem, as international trade brings more ships from more locations into regions where they had never before been. While laws have been passed that require ships to dump ballast water out at sea, they are often ignored, or the ballast is not completely cleaned out, so that small amounts of water are inadvertently released into lakes and rivers. Even a few small larvae in such ballast can enter the water, reproduce, and spread. Enormous amounts of money are spent in the United States to mitigate the problems brought about by invasive species and to attempt to keep new species from entering.

Toxic chemicals are continually released into the water, with new types and larger quantities being introduced each year. Some chemicals that were used with great disregard in the past have been banned because of the damage they caused to organisms and ecosystems. DDT is one such chemical. Although it did much good by reducing malaria and other insect-borne illnesses, the chemical accumulated at the top of the aquatic food web, causing birds such as bald eagles and peregrine falcons to lay eggs with thin shells, destroying their ability to reproduce. Despite the fact that it is a known environmental hazard, DDT continues to have limited use where malaria is still a problem because it is the most effective way to eliminate the mosquitoes that spread the disease. In this case, people have studied the cost-benefit analysis and determined that the small amount of DDT that enters the environment from this function is a price worth paying to control the spread of malaria.

Just as the link between DDT and reproduction problems in wildlife was straightforward, so are links between high levels of some toxic chemicals and health effects such as cancer in humans. However, linking health effects to a small amount of a single chemical is more difficult. Many cancers seem not to be linked to low exposures of a single chemical but, rather, may be the result of multiple chemicals in low exposures.

Tiny amounts of endocrine disruptors are beginning to be linked to gender problems in wildlife. Endocrine-disrupting chemicals found in sewage effluent are known to cause male fish to be feminized and female fish to be masculinized. Frogs are experiencing developmental problems, as well.

Endocrine-disrupting chemicals in the environment may be to blame for decreases in fertility, increases in testicular cancer, and changing sex ratios in human populations. While several chemicals have been taken off the market, or their use has been restricted, many more remain, and still more are being developed. Because these chemicals have been proliferating only since the 1940s, there are many things about them that we still do not know. We do not know what the human tolerance is for a single chemical or what the effects are of multiple chemicals working together. We do not know how people react to these chemicals in conjunction with other environmental stresses, and we do not know the effects that small cumulative doses have over one person's lifetime. What does seem true is that we are performing a giant experiment on ourselves and on the creatures sharing the planet with us. As is true with most first-time experiments, we do not know what the outcome will be.

Environmentalists favor using the precautionary principle to govern decisions where the outcome is questionable. They believe that the burden of proof must fall on those who favor the potentially harmful action. The two applications of the precautionary principle in the context of freshwater pollution are (1) chemical manufacturers must show that a compound is safe before it is used; and (2) a waste site should be cleaned up before it is shown to be harmful to people and wildlife. Chemical manufacturers and users, however, respond that the burden of proof should be on environmentalists to show that the chemical waste site is unsafe. The manufacturers and users point to the benefits of insecticides, plasticizers, and many other compounds, and to the costs of cleaning up waste sites. But with so little known about the effects of chemicals, particularly in the mixtures in which they are found in the environment, it seems prudent to take a more precautionary approach.

While by many measures the situation in the developed world is improving, the developing nations continue to face increasing problems as more people and higher standards of living lead to an increase in consumption and its byproduct, pollution. Developing economies do not want to take actions that may slow their growth, but maintaining long-term environmental and human health are indeed part of the cost of being a developed society. It is necessary for pollution to be regulated, monitored, and decreased in all parts of the world.

Awareness of environmental issues is rising. People are becoming better informed about the science behind the problems facing modern society and are making informed decisions regarding lifestyle choices. Education in schools and within communities will further this process.

Awareness of impact on all aspects of the environment by citizens could lead to change. As was stated by Debra Oliver, environmental inspector in King County, Washington, in an interview with *Waste News* in 2005, "Every dish I wash, every time I do my laundry, every time I take medication, every time I bathe my dog, I impact the environment. And when I impact the environment, it impacts you. And when you impact the environment, you impact me."

Individuals can reduce their consumption and vote with their pocketbooks by buying only necessary and environmentally friendly (or at least less damaging) products. Perhaps most importantly, people can bring their knowledge of these topics to bear when making political decisions, by supporting candidates who are more likely to implement policies that value the long-term future of the planet and who will work toward the adoption of those policies in the United States and internationally.

With education as to the needs of the world and its environment, with hope, and with enthusiasm, young people will play a major role in implementing change. The path the world is on can be changed, incrementally and completely, with knowledge, dedication, and determination.

Glossary

acid   A substance that releases hydrogen ions in solution; acidic solutions have numbers below 7 on the pH scale.

acid rain   Rainfall with a pH of less than 5.0. Acid rain is a type of acid precipitation, which includes acid fog and acid snow.

aerobic   Word used to describe an environment containing oxygen or an organism that breathes oxygen.

air pollution   Contamination of the air by particulates and toxic gases in concentrations that can endanger human and environmental health. Also known as smog.

alkaline   A solution in which hydroxyl ion is present in excess; alkaline solutions have numbers above 7 on the pH scale.

alien species   Organisms that are introduced by human activities into a location where they are not native; marine invasive species often travel in the ballast water of ships. Also known as invasive species.

alpine glacier   A glacier that grow in the mountains and flows downhill; at its source, snowfall exceeds snowmelt.

anaerobic   Word used to describe an oxygen-free environment or an organism, such as a bacterium, that lives in an oxygen-free environment.

androgen   A hormone that produces male characteristics. Testosterone, the principal androgen, is secreted by the testes to trigger the formation of male genitalia in the fetus and the maturation of the genitalia during adolescence.

anoxic   Without oxygen.

aquaculture The raising and harvesting of aquatic plants, fish, and shellfish in a water environment under controlled conditions.

aquifer A rock or soil layer that holds useable groundwater.

atom The smallest unit of a chemical element having the properties of that element.

atomic mass The sum of an atom's protons and neutrons (electrons have negligible weight).

bacteria Microscopic single-celled organisms that are important decomposers.

bioaccumulation The accumulation of toxic substances within living organisms.

biodegradable Word used to describe waste that living organisms can decompose into harmless inorganic materials; in some cases, such as with plastics, this process can take hundreds of years.

biodiversity The number of species in a given habitat.

bioremediation The use of microbes, such as bacteria, to break down hazardous wastes.

bog A small lake without an inlet or outlet and with characteristic vegetation including sphagnum moss, which may coat the surface and supply a foothold for other plants.

brackish Word used to describe water with a salinity between that of fresh water and ocean water.

cancer A group of more than 100 distinct diseases that are typified by the uncontrolled growth of abnormal cells in the body.

carcinogen A substance that causes cancer. Carcinogens affect people with a genetic predisposition for getting the disease more than those without that disposition, except in cases of extreme exposure to the carcinogen.

chemical bond Mechanism by which atoms come together to form molecules; chemical bonds must be strong enough to keep the atoms together as an aggregate.

cholera An often fatal disease caused by a bacterium and spread through fecal matter.

condensation The change in state of a substance from a gas to a liquid.

continental divide A geographic feature from which the water on either side flows toward different oceans.

continental glacier A mass of ice that moves outward from a center of accumulation. Also known as an ice cap.

covalent bond Strong chemical bond in which atoms share electrons.

cryptosporidiosis An intestinal disease caused by the parasite cryptosporidium.

dead zone A region in a body of water that is hostile to most life, usually due to eutrophication.

decomposer An organism that breaks down the body parts of dead organisms or their waste into nutrients that can be used by other plants and animals.

degraded water Water that is not suitable for drinking because it contains natural or human-made contamination.

dioxin A toxic chemical that is a byproduct of the manufacture of other chemicals and that has been shown to be hazardous to animals and possibly humans; it is considered a persistent organic pollutant (POP).

divide A rock ridge that separates two drainages.

drainage basin A river and all of its tributaries and all of the land that it drains.

ecosystem The interrelationships of the plants and animals of a region and the raw materials that they need to live.

ectotherm An animal whose body temperature is the same as its surrounding environment; also called "cold blooded."

electrons Negatively-charged particles that orbit an atom's nucleus.

element   A substance that cannot be chemically reduced to simpler substances.

endocrine disruptor   A compound that interrupts the functions of the endocrine system, often interfering with the sexual development or success of a species; most endocrine disruptors are estrogens or estrogen mimics.

endocrine system   The system of the body that controls the internal environment by sending out hormones as chemical messengers.

endotherm   An animal that uses food energy to fuel its body temperature, which remains nearly constant without being affected by the temperature of its environment; also called "warm blooded."

ephemeral stream   A stream that flows only part of the year, usually during the rainy season.

epidemic   A disease outbreak that affects more people than is normal for that disease or that spreads to regions where it does not normally occur.

epidemiology   Field of medicine concerned with the study of epidemics. Unlike medical doctors who deal with disease in individuals, epidemiologists deal with disease in populations.

estrogen   Vertebrate female sex hormone that regulates the reproductive cycle and the development of the sex organs.

eutrophic   A nutrient-rich lake that supports a great deal of algae; its waters are oxygen poor.

eutrophication   The changes that occur in an aquatic ecosystem when excessive nutrients are released; commonly, the depletion of oxygen by bacteria.

evaporation   The change of state of a substance from a liquid to a gas, such as the change from liquid water to water vapor.

evapotranspiration   The loss of water by evaporation from plants.

feminization   The process by which a male organism takes on the traits of a female; this may occur after exposure to female sex hormones or their mimics.

flash flood   A sudden rush of water down a valley that is caused by heavy rainfall, sometimes miles from where the flood does its greatest damage.

floodplain   Level land along a stream formed by the deposition of sediments during flooding.

food web   The overlapping of food chains to form a web that make up the biological portion of an ecosystem.

fossil fuels   Ancient plants that have decayed and been transformed into a useable fuel, especially coal and petroleum. These fuels are really just stored ancient sunshine.

geothermal energy   Energy that comes from hot water; this water is heated in a volcano or in the deep Earth.

glacier   A moving mass of ice and snow that forms on land. Glaciers grow when the amount of snow falling in winter exceeds the amount that melts in spring and summer, and they shrink when annual snowmelt exceeds snowfall.

greenhouse gases   Gases that absorb heat radiated from the Earth. They include carbon dioxide, methane, ozone, nitrous oxide, and chlorofluorocarbons.

groundwater   Water found in soil or rock beneath the ground surface.

headwater   The location where a stream begins, usually in high mountains.

heavy metal   A metal with high weight, especially one that is toxic to organisms.

hydrocarbon   An organic compound composed of hydrogen and carbon; fossil fuels are hydrocarbons.

hydropower   The potential energy of falling water; it can be harnessed by a waterwheel, or at a waterfall or hydroelectric dam.

hydrosphere   The watery parts of the Earth, including atmospheric water vapor, oceans, ice caps, glaciers, lakes, ponds, streams, groundwater, and clouds.

hydrogen bond A weak chemical bond in which the positive side of one polar molecule is attracted to the negative side of another polar molecule.

hydrologic cycle The cycling of water between Earth's atmosphere, oceans, and freshwater reservoirs such as glaciers, streams, lakes, and groundwater aquifers.

hypoxic Word used to describe water containing little or no free oxygen.

ice cap A mass of ice that moves outward from a center of accumulation; currently, Earth has two ice caps, in Greenland and Antarctica. Also known as a continental glacier.

invasive species Organisms that are introduced by human activities into a location where they are not native; marine invasive species often travel in the ballast water of ships. Also known as alien species.

ion An atom that has lost or gained an electron so that it has a positive or negative charge.

ionic bond Chemical bond in which one atom gives one or more electrons to another atom.

invertebrate An animal without a backbone.

isotope Two or more atoms of the same element having the same number of protons but a different number of neutrons; that is, a different atomic mass number.

kinetic energy The energy describing a body in motion.

marsh A low wetland, often treeless but covered with grasses, periodically covered with water.

masculinization The process by which a female organism takes on masculine traits, which may occur if the organism is exposed to male sex hormones or their mimics.

metabolite What is left of a compound, such as a drug, after it is altered by body processes.

molecular weight The sum of the weights of all the atoms in a molecule.

molecule   The smallest unit of a compound that has all the properties of that compound.

neutrons   Uncharged subatomic particles found in an atom's nucleus.

non-point source pollution   Pollution that comes from a large area such as an urbanized region or the atmosphere.

nonrenewable resource   A resource that is not replenished on a time-scale that is useful to humans, so that when it is gone, there is no more; petroleum and many mineral resources are nonrenewable.

nucleus   The center of an atom, composed of protons and neurons.

nutrients   Biologically important elements that are critical to growth or to building shells or bones; nitrates, phosphorus, carbonate, and silicate are some of the nutrients that are important for marine organisms.

oligotrophic   A lake that is nutrient poor and so has clear, blue water and little plant life; the waters are oxygen rich.

oocyst   The inactive form of a microbe; oocysts can persist in the environment under harsh conditions and so can survive wastewater treatment and other processes designed to eliminate them.

overfishing   A situation in which too many fish are being taken from a fishery so that the fish population cannot replenish itself.

pathogens   Microorganisms—primarily bacteria, viruses, parasites, and toxic algae—that cause disease.

PCBs (polychlorinated biphenyls)   Extremely stable, water soluble, persistent organic pollutants that bioaccumulate and are found globally.

peat   Organic matter formed by incompletely decayed plant bodies; peat is found in bogs.

perennial stream   A stream that flows continually, independent of the season.

permafrost   Permanently frozen soil; it is common in the polar regions.

permeability   The interconnectedness of the pores and cracks in a rock or soil layer; the pores in a permeable layer are highly interconnected so that groundwater can move easily through it.

persistent organic pollutants (POPs)   Chemical substances that persist in the environment, bioaccumulate through the food web, and may damage human health and the environment.

pH   Numbers from 0 to 14 that express the acidity or alkalinity of a solution. On the pH scale, 7 is neutral, with lower numbers indicating acid and higher numbers indicating base. The most extreme numbers are the most extreme solutions.

photosynthesis   The process in which plants use carbon dioxide and water to produce sugar and oxygen. The simplified chemical reaction is $6CO_2 + 12H_2O +$ solar energy $= C_6H_{12}O_6 + 6O_2 + 6H_2O$.

phytoplankton   Microscopic plantlike, usually single-celled, organisms found at the surface of an ocean or lake; they are the planet's single greatest source of oxygen.

plasticizers   Additives that soften the material they are added to, often plastics and usually PVC. Some common plasticizers are classified as toxic chemicals by the EPA.

point source pollution   Pollution that can be traced to a single source, such as a pipe or tank.

polar molecule   A molecule in which one side has a positive charge and the other a negative charge; water is a polar molecule.

pollutants   Artificial impurities that are found in the environment. Freshwater pollutants include plastics, oil, heat, pharmaceuticals, and nutrients.

porosity   The spaces in a rock or soil layer; a rock with good porosity can hold a lot of water.

precipitation   Condensed moisture that falls to the ground as rain, sleet, hail, snow, frost, or dew.

primary productivity   The food energy created by producers.

protons   Positively charged subatomic particles found in an atom's nucleus.

reclaimed water   Water from a wastewater treatment plant, or water that has been used in another industrial process.

remediation   The process of cleaning up pollutants.

renewable resource   A resource that is capable of regeneration; hydro-electric power is a renewable resource.

reservoir   (1) A part of the Earth system where water is found, including the atmosphere, oceans, lakes, streams, ponds, and groundwater. (2) An artificial pond or lake created by a dam and used for storing water.

riparian corridor   The ribbon of plants lining a stream that depend on the stream for nutrients, water, and organic material; the plants in the riparian corridor are different from those farther away from the stream.

runoff   Water that trickles across roadways and rooftops; runoff also filters through landfills and soil and often drains directly into streams or lakes.

saline   Water containing salt.

salinization   The increase in salt content in soil due to irrigating it with brackish water.

schistosomiasis   Parasitic disease caused by blood flukes, which need water for part of their life cycle.

sediment   Fragments of rocks and minerals that range in size from dust and clay up to the size of boulders. Freshwater sediment serves as a feeding ground for various species.

seiche   A stationary wave in an enclosed or semi-enclosed water body such as a lake.

sewage   Material that passes through sewers, including what is flushed down toilets, runs down sinks, and passes from gutters into sewer holes.

sewage sludge   The material that remains when the water is removed from sewage; sewage sludge includes human and animal waste, pathogens, toxic chemicals, and other materials.

spawn   A mass of eggs laid by some species of female fish and invertebrates.

spring A water source where a groundwater aquifer intercepts the surface.

stream Any moving water, from a rivulet to the world's largest river.

stygobionts Tiny creatures, mostly invertebrates, that live between the grains in groundwater aquifers and in landforms created by groundwater.

subsidence Sinking of the land surface due to the collapse of pore spaces in an aquifer after the groundwater is removed.

Superfund A law passed in 1980 and more formally known as the Comprehensive Environmental Response, Compensation, and Liability Act (CERCLA), Superfund provides financial assistance with removal of contaminated materials and helps pay for remedial action during cleanup over the long term.

sustainable Resource use that does not compromise the current needs for resources or the resources that will be needed by future generations for present economic gain.

swamp Poorly drained regions where the water table lies above the ground surface.

thermal pollution Waste heat from industrial processes or roadways that raises the temperature of the aquatic environment.

tide The regular rise and fall of sea or lake level due to the gravitational forces exerted by the Moon and Sun on the Earth.

trachoma Infection of the mucous membrane of the eyelids caused by the bacterium *Chlamydia trachomatis,* which is the second leading cause of blindness after cataracts. Spread of the disease is easily reduced by washing in clean water.

tributary A smaller stream that flows into a larger stream.

tributyltin (TBT) A tin-containing compound that is an effective anti-fouling agent and an endocrine disruptor.

turnover An increase in the density of the water at the surface of a lake so that the surface water sinks, allowing the deeper water to rise; this process brings dissolved oxygen into the deeper portion of the lake.

water pollution Contamination of the waterways (surface or groundwater) due to human activities.

watershed A river and all of its tributaries and all of the land that it drains.

water table The top of an aquifer; above the water table, pore spaces are filled with air and infiltrating water; below the water table, the pore spaces are filled with water.

water vapor Water (H_2O) in its gaseous state.

waterway Streams, lakes, and ponds, especially when they are linked together.

wetlands Poorly drained regions that are covered all or part of the time with fresh or salt water.

zooplankton Tiny marine animals that are unable to swim on their own and that drift with the currents.

Further Reading

Barringer, Felicity. "Billions Needed to Improve Great Lakes, Coalition Says." *The New York Times*, July 8, 2005.

———. "A Search for Pearls of Wisdom in the Matter of Swine." *The New York Times*, July 7, 2004.

Beardslee, G. William. "The 1832 Cholera Epidemic in New York State: 19th Century Responses to *Cholerae Vibrio*." Archiving Early America. Available online. URL: http://earlyamerica.com/review/2000_fall/1832_cholera.html#_edn16. Accessed April 27, 2007.

Beck, Eckardt C. "The Love Canal Tragedy." U.S. Environmental Protection Agency. Available online. URL: http://www.epa.gov/history/topics/lovecanal/01.htm. Accessed April 27, 2007.

Bennett, Elena, and Steve R. Carpenter. "P Soup: It's Green, But It's Not Good for You. That Benign-Looking Pond Scum Signifies A Far-Reaching Shift In The Global Phosphorus Cycle." *World Watch* 15 (March, 2002): 24–33.

Burdick, Alan. *Out of Eden: An Odyssey of Ecological Invasion*. New York: Farrar, Straus, and Giroux, 2005.

Carson, Rachel. *Silent Spring*. New York: Houghton Mifflin Company, 1962.

Colburn, T., D. Dumanoski, and J.P. Myers. *Our Stolen Future: How We Are Threatening Our Fertility, Intelligence and Survival*. New York: Plume, 1997.

Cushman, John H., Jr. "Pollution by Factory Farms Inspires Industrial Approach to Regulation." *The New York Times*, March 6, 1998.

Daly, Gay. "Bad Chemistry." OnEarth. Natural Resources Defense Council. Available online. URL: http://www.nrdc.org/onearth/06win/chem1.asp. Accessed April 27, 2007.

Daunton, Martin. "London's Great Stink: The Sour Smell of Success." BBC-History. Available online. URL: http://www.bbc.co.uk/history/lj/ victorian_britainlj/smell_of_success_4.shtml?site=history_victorianlj_ sour. Accessed April 27, 2007.

Editorial. "How to Poison a River." *The New York Times*, August 19, 2005.

Egan, Dan. "Zebra Mussels Among Invasive Species Harming Lake Michigan." *Milwaukee Journal Sentinel* (via Knight-Ridder/Tribune News Service), January 3, 2005.

Environmental Protection Agency (EPA). Clean Water Act. Available online: http://www.epa.gov/region5/water/cwa.htm. Accessed April 27, 2007.

————. "Energy Star." Available online. URL: http://www.energystar.gov/. Accessed April 27, 2007.

————. "Enviroene: Common Sense Solutions to Environmental Problems." Available online. URL: http://es.epa.gov/. Accessed April 27, 2007.

————. "The Great Lakes: An Environmental Atlas and Resource Book." Available online. URL: http://www.epa.gov/glnpo/atlas/index.html. Accessed April 27, 2007.

————. "Green vehicle guide." Available online. URL: http://www.epa. gov/autoemissions/. Accessed April 27, 2007.

————. "Superfund: Cleaning Up the Nation's Hazardous Waste Sites." Available online. URL: http://www.epa.gov/superfund/. Accessed April 27, 2007.

————. "Toxic Air Pollutants." Available online. http://www.epa.gov/air/ toxicair/index.html. Accessed April 27, 2007.

Geisel, Theodor Seuss. *The Lorax, by Dr. Seuss*. New York: Random House, 1971.

Harr, Jonathan. *A Civil Action*. New York: Random House, 1995.

Johnson, Jim. "Problems Just Begin When Pills Flush Down the Drain." *Waste News* 11 (May 23, 2005): 15–16.

Johnson, N., C. Revenga, and J. Echeverria. "Managing Water for People and Nature." *Science* 292 (May, 2001): 1071.

Kilgannon, Corey. "Hook, Line and Sinker." *The New York Times*, June 6, 1999.

Larson, Lee. "The Great USA Flood of 1993." Available online. URL: http://www.nwrfc.noaa.gov/floods/papers/oh_2/great.htm. Accessed April 27, 2007.

Mohn, Tanya. "When Runoff Flows Untreated." *The New York Times*, February 2, 2003.

Morell, Virginia. "The Fragile World of Frogs." *National Geographic* 199 (May, 2001): 106.

Nierenberg, Danielle. "Toxic Fertility." *World Watch* 14 (March, 2001): 30.

Pelton, Tom. "Drug Traces Found in Water Pose Problem for Wildlife." *Baltimore Sun*, October 16, 2005.

Perkins, S. "Steep Degrade Ahead: Road Salt Threatens Waters in Northeast." *Science News* 168 (September, 2005): 195–196.

Rosenberg, Charles E. *The Cholera Years: The United States in 1832, 1849, and 1866.* Chicago: The University of Chicago Press, 1962.

Travis, J. "Mussel Muzzled: Bacterial Toxin May Control Pest." *Science News* 161 (June, 2002): 339–340.

Urbina, Ian. "A Gasoline Additive Lingers in New York's Drinking Water." *The New York Times*, October 31, 2004.

World Wildlife Fund. "Causes for Concern: Chemicals and Wildlife." Available online. URL: http://assets.panda.org/downloads/causesforconcern.pdf. Accessed April 27, 2007.

WEB SITES

Everglades National Park
http://www.nps.gov/ever/
Flora, fauna, and geology of the Everglades.

Hetch Hetchy Reclaimed
http://www.sacbee.com/content/opinion/story/10638026p-11432525c.html
The Sacramento Bee's Pulitzer Prize–winning series about the Hetch Hetchy Valley.

Our Stolen Future
http://www.ourstolenfuture.org
Recent developments in the field of endocrine disruption by the authors of the book Our Stolen Future.

Rachel Carson

http://www.rachelcarson.org

The life and legacy of Rachel Carson.

Sierra Club

http://www.sierraclub.org

The environmental organization started by John Muir.

Water on the Web

http://waterontheweb.org

Web site devoted to training students to understand and solve real-world environmental problems; includes primers on lake ecology, stream ecology, and watersheds.

Index

About the Author

DANA DESONIE, PH.D., has written about earth, ocean, space, life, and environmental sciences for more than a decade. Her work has appeared in educational lessons, textbooks, and magazines and on radio and the Web. Her 1996 book, *Cosmic Collisions*, described the importance of asteroids and comets in Earth history and the possible consequences of a future asteroid collision with the planet. Before becoming a science writer, she received a doctorate in oceanography, spending weeks at a time at sea, mostly in the tropics, and one amazing day at the bottom of the Pacific in the research submersible *Alvin*. She now resides in Phoenix, Arizona, with her neuroscientist husband, Miles Orchinik, and their two children.